UNLEASHED

A Woman's Guide To Uncover Her Inner Power

SUZANA PIRES

Published by WeBook Publishing
All rights in the English language reserved.
No portion of this book may be copied, stored in recovery systems, or transferred by any means, whether electronic or mechanical, nor photocopied, recorded, or otherwise, without the author's and the Publisher's written permission.

Copyright © 2023 Suzana Pires
First Hardcover Edition
Foreword © 2023 Sharon Stone
ISBN: 978-1-7372780-8-5
LCCN: 2023941168
Written by Suzana Pires
Copy Editor: Ana Silvani
Foreword by: Sharon Stone
Cover Design: Drica Lobo
Cover Photo: Luciana Dalri
Photo Makeup: Krishna Carvalho
Photo Styling: Renato Pinhel
Figures: Clara Soria
Interior Layout: Jahid Munshi
Translated by: Dayse Boechat & Ana Silvani
Manufactured in the United States of America

Pires, Suzana, author. Unleashed : a woman's guide to uncover her inner power / Suzana Pires, Ana Silvani, WeBook Publishing. First english edition. Los Angeles : WeBook Publishing, 2023.
1.Women in Business 2. Self-Help 3. Entrepreneurship 4. Motivational

Note

Much care and technique were employed in editing this book. However, there can be no assurance that it will be free of minor typing errors, printing issues, or even conceptual ambivalence. In any such case, we ask that the issue be notified to our customer service at the e-mail address:
info@webookpublishing.com

ENGLISH EDITION
WEBOOK PUBLISHING

To my parents, Maria Elizabete Carvalho and João Felippe Pires, for their efforts to provide me with the best education possible.

The following is based on a true story:

In a bustling office of a major company, a conversation went down like this:

Boss: We have some feedback on your work.

Me: Sure, lay it on me so I can up my game. I'm all ears.

Boss: Well, here's the thing. You're way too cheerful.

Me: (speechless)

Boss: With all your infectious cheerfulness, you manage to get your team to do whatever you ask.

Me: (speechless)

Boss: But the downside is that you end up cutting corners, skipping over important processes.

Me: Let me get this straight: the company wants me to tone down my happiness.

Boss: We want anything but that.

Me: Well, sorry to burst your bubble, but settling for average is not my thing.

Six months later, the contract was terminated after a remarkable 10-year partnership. The journey recounted in this book became a reality thanks to the "Dona de Si" (Unleashed) brand's actions and institute.

That was when I realized who I had become and the non-negotiables for me. Now, let's try to understand your story, shall we?

FROM THE AUTHOR

As a child, I wasn't exactly the reserved, single-minded type, so my parents felt the need to pinpoint the qualities I seemed to be "missing" and encourage me to develop them to some extent. In order to instill discipline, they enrolled me in rhythmic gymnastics because it was a highly competitive sport. To broaden my horizons and embrace the world as an expansive territory, I embarked on a journey of language learning, was immersed in diverse experiences, and gained a deeper understanding of different cultures. I studied in a public school and forged friendships with classmates from different backgrounds, beliefs, and social standings. The school was *Colégio* Pedro II, where the student body ranges from the sons and daughters of company presidents to students that depend on the donation of the school uniform.

At Pedro II, everyone was alike. No special treatment was given to the "whiter" or the "richer." Not at all. I never saw that happen during my school years. Quite the contrary: we all had to follow the rules, keep our grade point average up, and not fail. Otherwise, we would have to find another school.

By the end of secondary school, I had already worked as an actress, and the deal I had with my parents was: I could choose whatever university course I wanted as long as I studied hard. So, I chose to take philosophy, which added so much value to my career as an actress and as an author. Later, I felt the need for an education in management, as it had become clear to me that my career would not take off unless I managed it myself. So, I attended the United Nations (UN) course for entrepreneurs, which was delivered in Brazil by Sebrae. This was in addition to the acting courses offered by Camilla Amado, and Fátima Toledo, the famous acting courses of Tablado and Théâtre du Soleil, the screenwriting courses organized by John Truby, José Carvalho, Eliseu Altunaga, and Guilhermo Arriaga, besides the ShowRunner Drama Series, in Los Angeles.

Yes, I have always studied hard; that makes me feel I have a solid background. Even when I fail or cannot fully dominate a given subject. Because my learning muscles are exercised constantly, I have no problem saying, "I don't know how to do it," which provides me with a special power: understanding that vulnerability is something that drives my strength.

For my parents' upbringing – which allowed me to grow into a professional in constant pursuit of excellence, a woman who owns her life, and a person with so much love for other people – I am extremely grateful!

FOREWORD

The central posit in Suzan Pires book UNLEASHED is: can we allow ourselves our own freedom, and if so, can you take this journey to get there? Freedom from what and for what purpose, we ask, or do we just know?

This is the text of Suzan's personal journey to find that very path. At this particular time in history, we are all once again pushing through the socio-political question of our own value and worth. The meaning of our own human purpose. Are we, as women, simply here to serve the male agenda?

If so, why and for what deeper exchange? Does the individual sense of purpose have value and meaning in these constructs? And if so, if that individual is female, how can that purpose and value be realized? If that person is male, is this moment reaching his genuine hopes and dreams?

Ms. Pires sets a course for her own life and shares her journey step by step as a template for this journey while charting a course that is easily understood, well-defined and expressed with loving authority. She is a champion for women and girls. These are daunting times no matter who one may be or the circumstances of one's life as we have seen and experienced the backsliding of our human rights and in particular the rights of women and girls on a global scale.

This is a time for a raising of our own sense of pride of self; knowing the power of communication that we share while bonding in our natural strengths. It is imperative that we recognize our ability to become a group who are one simply because we are; this must be at the forefront of our consciousness.

If you find that this book is your map, your way forward, then brava, for we are all walking to a new frontier, if not, pass it to the correct friend and we will see you down the path; where we all walk together, UNLEASHED.

Kindest regards,
Sharon Stone

Sharon Stone is an Oscar-nominated American actress known for roles in movies such as *Basic Instinct*, *Casino*, and *Lovelace*. She won a Golden Globe for her exceptional performance in the movie *Casino*.

THANK YOU

To my sister, Giselia Carvalho, my brother-in-law, Eduardo Brasil, and my Goddaughter, Gabi, for all the love, for listening, and for all your motivation!

To my friends and your fabulous contributions to my life: Kevin Gssay, Chuck James, Gil Titzu, Josh Khan, Mariana Jorge, Talize Sayeg, Viviane Duarte, Bruno Astuto, Bruno Chateaubriand, Luana Xavier, Cristiano Pio de Almeida, Maythe Birman, Renato Santos, Maria Maya, Cande Salles, Katie Elmore Mota, Mauricio Mota and Thalita Rebouças.

To my professional coach, Virginia de Gomez; my publisher in the U.S., Ana Silvani; my manager in Brazil, Marcus Montenegro (@montenegrotalents), and to my manager in the U.S., Ben Pollack @braveartistsmanagement for your unrelenting trust in the quality that I deliver.

To Marina Caruso, for inviting me to write a column for Marie Claire Brazil magazine, which became the column "DONA DE SI" (UNLEASHED).

To Daniela Falcão, former CEO of Editora Globo/Conde Nast, which publishes VOGUE Brazil, which formerly published the column "DONA DE SI" (UNLEASHED), I thank you for the courage to share this subject matter with your readers and for trusting me with it. To Forbes Woman Online, which published the column "DONA DE SI" (UNLEASHED), thank you for your trust.

TABLE OF CONTENTS

Introduction 1

Part 1 5
    The Seed To Becoming Unleashed 8
    Education 9
    Experience 12

Part 2 15
    Step 1 – Developing Resilience 19
    Experience 25
    Step 2 – Building Independence (Paying Your Bills) 32
    Protagonism 41
    Goals 42
    Purpose 47
    Building A New Image On Top Of My Work As An Actress . 52
    Step 3 – How To Build Teams And Make It Work With Diverse People 53
    Sense Of Belonging 57
    The Big Challenge Of Leadership 59
    Step 4 – What Have I Learned After So Many Struggles? ... 65
    Step 5 – What Am I Going To Leave To The World? 69
    The Story Behind The Sale Of The Chanel Handbags ... 71
    "Dona De Si" (Unleashed) Is In Fashion 73
    Unleashed + Arezzo 75

- Getting Back To The Institute's Day-To-Day Impact 76
- Maslow Pyramid 78
- Sisterhood 79
- Point 1: The World's Money Is Not Going To Run Out 85
- Point 2: Our Worst Enemy Is Despair 86
- Point 3: What Is The New Strategy? 87
- How Can We Hack The System? 88
- Multiplying 90
- Expanding My Territory 94
- Let's Get Practical 98
- Female Overburden, Oppression, And Loneliness 99

Part 3 105
- Make A Commitment To Yourself 105
- Our Fellow Females, Our Stories 106
- When The Study With My Readers Was Finished… 116
- Test To Identify Your Persona 118
- Persona Test Result 122
- Learning To Be A Protagonist 139
- Now It Is Your Turn 164
- Commitment Contract With Myself 165

Part 4 168
- Meet Some Of Our Unleashed Women 168

About The Author 172

Bibliography 173

INTRODUCTION

A FEW THINGS BEFORE WE START

This book is an invitation for you to uncover your inner power and become UNLEASHED. However, for you to feel comfortable deciding to come on this journey with me, I should make a few points clear:

POINT ZERO

What qualifies me to help you become UNLEASHED?

My professional journey makes me well-suited to write this book. However, I don't want you to read what's ahead and think: "Here comes another book about how I should behave." That is not what I want, and I will not do that. Quite the contrary: This book will encourage you to be authentic.

POINT ONE

What does it mean to be UNLEASHED?

It means being a free and independent woman who views herself as her own personal enterprise.

POINT TWO

What is the importance of being UNLEASHED?

The goal is to create a job market and a business world of freer and more independent women who are protagonists and face the limitations imposed by the male-dominated market.

POINT THREE

What happens when you become UNLEASHED?

By accepting the invitation to show your true self to the world, you will be forced to face your inner weaknesses, those flaws that prevent you from fully exploring your talents. This will help you to identify your qualities to become the protagonist of your own life.

POINT FOUR

What will we be fighting?

This is not a battle of sexes but a realization and awakening of our position in the dynamics of power.

POINT FIVE

What is my goal?

- Help you identify what is holding you back.
- Unlock your progress.

POINT SIX

What happens when it doesn't work out in the end?

The measure of success is within yourself, and it comes in stages, takes time, and requires a solid foundation of mental health. When you prioritize yourself and your goals, the possibilities are endless, and you will succeed - there's no other way.

POINT SEVEN

Will you be able to contact me when you need to?

Yes! I am available through the following channels:

Instagram:

@unleashedfoundation

@institutodonadesi

@suzipires

PART 1

SUZI,
WERE YOU BORN UNLEASHED?

Simone de Beauvoir, French essayist and fictional author, wrote the notorious phrase "One is not born a woman: one becomes a woman" in The Second Sex (1949), a book that inspired the feminist movement in the 1960s. In it, the author examines this "becoming a woman" process in post-War France and how female subordination manifests in this context.

Paraphrasing Simone, I often say that I was born a woman but became an unleashed woman, in control of my own life, after embarking on a long journey. In this book, you'll have the opportunity to follow along and witness this transformative path firsthand.

I launched this book in Brazil in March 2022 with tremendous success and embarked on a speaking tour where the attendance was never short of 500 women. Then, in August of 2022, I received an exciting publishing proposal from Ana Silvani, the editor of WeBook, to release the book in the USA. At first, I was ecstatic about the opportunity to connect with women from different nationalities. But, of course, my inner critic surfaced, and I became paralyzed. I couldn't write a single line for this English version. Until I received the feedback from the beta-read commentaries. With each note, I got to know my readers and understood where we could share experiences and new ideas.

Sure, there are differences in the daily realities between women living in developed countries and those living in developing nations. However, much to my surprise, there is hardly any disparity between our mental states and self-beliefs. The patriarchy has managed to forge leashes for women from all walks of life. I felt fully prepared to initiate this dialogue with you by identifying their restraints.

We are battling against the same invisible limits imposed by the system, whether we are Brazilian, Mexican, Japanese, or American.

I also have to mention my coach, Virginia de Gomez, who organized the tests and practices you will find here. I am delighted and proud that this book before you is the product of these Brazilian women's happy encounters and combined strength.

I become increasingly convinced with each passing day that success comes with its fair share of countless failures. Therefore, our lives revolve around finding that delicate balance - to understand what it truly means to be alive, stepping into the arena, and engaging in the fight. I can assure you that achieving success is far from being a walk in the park. It's not all sunshine, roses, or gold medals, as some would have us believe. There is no magic formula.

Success means facing our demons and praising ourselves for having the courage to do it. It means being terrified of something and doing it anyway. Success is acknowledging our mistakes, learning from them, and making another attempt once we have analyzed and changed what went wrong. It means taking risks, reshaping ourselves, and changing our own souls as well as the souls of those around us.

In this book, I will tell you how I, a girl from Rio de Janeiro, in a middle-class family, without any connection to the arts, made my own way to working as an actress, became an author, a businesswoman, the creator of the "Dona de Si" (UNLEASHED) brand, the founder of "Dona de Si" Institute in Brazil, and now, a Brazilian artist in Hollywood.

I will show you how you, too, can make your journey a success, regardless of the phase you are in now. And, if you want, I will help you take the first steps until you feel comfortable walking alone. Because, after all, I want to – and I know that I will – see you shine!

THE SEED TO BECOMING UNLEASHED

Since childhood, my biggest pleasure was making up stories and bringing them to life. I would use the balcony at my grandparents' house, in Araruama, a lagoon town in the State of Rio de Janeiro, as a stage. My family and neighbors were my audiences, and my friends and cousins were the cast. Naturally, I was the writer and the director and played the main character. All of that without a care in the world if anyone thought I was being selfish, presumptuous, or bossy. That was how we played, and it came together instinctively. My cousin Marcelo was in charge of the soundtrack, which consisted of music and sounds he made using home objects. A friend improvised outfits, and we had a lot of fun.

In my pre-adolescent phase, some people started saying that I laughed too loud, that I should wear shorts under my skirt, that my movements were too extravagant, and, for everything that I wanted to do, I would have to explain myself to one person or another. There. It did not take long for the chaos of adolescence to take hold of my life - a phase that I would only depart from as an authentic young woman or a castrated woman.

My parents were never backward people, but they are who they are, and I am who I am, right? So, it was only natural, especially during my teenage years, that we would have different world views and conflicting beliefs. While my desire to be an artist grew, their concern grew just as much. They would say: "You need to have a real job, a salary to pay your bills in order to work as an artist." Now, I understand and respect them. But, back then, the only thing I could do was rebel and try to negotiate my choices, proving that I knew what I wanted to achieve and that I was not clueless and irresponsible.

I used to enjoy those negotiations, and today I understand why: the exercise of committing to certain arrangements and choices made me a person of my word, someone who saw things through and did them with total dedication. That is not to say that it was easy. We had many conflicts and endless conversations until I could finally emerge as the entrepreneur of my own life.

EDUCATION

Missing class or dropping out of school was non-negotiable in our home. When I started studying theater at Tablado at the age of 15, I failed the 11th grade and started to question the need to stay in school. It was one of the worst moments of my life and the most difficult with my family. I finished high school because I had to. When the time came to take my college admission exams, I was rehearsing for a professional play I was being paid to do. But I had made a deal with my parents and had to dedicate equal time to the rehearsals and to my studies. The result: I barely slept or ate.

My lifelong determination to juggle multiple things at once started there and the result was not great: my performance in the admission exams was terrible. I didn't mark an X on a single question because I passed out when the inspector said, "You can now flip the test over and begin."

I experienced burnout. That was my very first blackout caused by sheer physical and mental exhaustion. Looking back, I realize that the notion that I am vulnerable – like all human beings – makes me a woman that is more comfortable with herself. The role of the protagonist of one's own story requires deep self-awareness. It includes, above all, dealing with our limits. But little did I know back then.

That incident during the admission exam showed everyone how committed I was. It was the first time I felt myself, my sense of discipline and responsibility, and my excesses.

My parents agreed to forget about the admission test, at least for the time being, so that I could dedicate my full attention to the play. We toured all over Brazil, and I experienced being a professional artist just like I always wanted to. Even though I found out that giving interviews wasn't all about glamour, I still knew that was what I wanted for my life. I confirmed my desire and started making choices to support my dreams.

The following year, I decided to start college and chose to major in Philosophy. I loved those classes and knew they would add knowledge to my work as a professional actress and an aspiring author. As a passionate person, I applied my enthusiasm to everything I was learning about in the dramatic works of the time and in my philosophy classes to match art and thinking. That was when I started my studies about philosophical plays. Side note: you would never think that the character *Glorinha*, "the woman in the window," from the soap opera *Gabriela*, have studied that, would you? (*Gabriela*, a popular Brazilian soap opera from the 70s, was revived in a reboot in 2012).

Besides being an artist, I wanted to become the woman I was born to be. And I always knew that would be a daily battle.

When I was 14, my parents gifted me with the "feminist bible" by Simone de Beauvoir: The Second Sex, which I have mentioned before. Yes, an engineer and a lawyer gifted me with that book. I believe my parents already knew who their daughter was going to be and decided to contribute to her feminist education. That way, I could take my cause seriously instead of just spewing out the jargon.

To this day, I think the strong but silent dialog that ensued between my father (a guy with a deep voice and a mustache from the male generation that smoked and drank whiskey) and me was fantastic. That man, João Felippe, was observing me and preparing me for the time when I would have to fight the world instead of him. During my teen years, when he saw me laughing loudly and expressing my joy, he understood who I was. And, I assure you, a father understanding his daughter is very important, a sublime blessing. He focused on what really mattered: guiding me to the best version of myself. Oh, Dad, you are such a great guy.

On the other hand, my mother showed me that age would never be a limitation in my life. She fulfilled her dream of becoming a lawyer after 40, and that was one of my biggest inspirations during my teen years. My sister, who is seven years older, has always been committed to her achievements as well: at 16, she had already worked for a major corporation as an electronics technician. I constantly noticed her being the only woman in her work department – which made me never feel intimidated when faced with the dynamic of being the only woman in workspaces.

I understood early on that trying to please people and belonging to the status quo were unimportant to me. I was going to write my own story (in fact, I had already started doing so) on my terms, based on my choices, not on "traditional rules" trying to hold me back. When I made this decision, my life started to flow more easily. I began engaging in activities with people who did not judge me for "being different." Quite the contrary: they instigated me to explore other facets of life.

EXPERIENCE

At 17, while studying Philosophy, I experienced a new platform for my work as an actress: television. I was hired by *TV Manchete* (the Brazilian network remained on air from 1983 to 1999) to join the cast of the soap opera *Tocaia Grande*, based on the novel of the same name by Brazilian author Jorge Amado, and directed by Regis Cardoso and later on, by Walter Avancini.

I enjoyed the television dynamic of taping in a studio and on a city set. I learned a great deal from the other cast members but hated the power relations that were in place there. I've worked with a famous Brazilian director who was abusive. Every time I was in the studio and felt an uncomfortable hand around my waist, it was him: that creepy old man who constantly tried to hit on a 17-year-old girl. I wanted to push him away and give him a punch in the face, but I had to restrain myself and put on a fake smile.

Back in 1994, women's rights, especially for actresses, weren't as recognized as they are today. I despised his behavior but had no one to confide in. Within 6 months of working there, I had gained about 10 pounds due to stress (that pesky hormone can make you bloated and heavier). On top of that, I experienced hair loss and developed a strange allergic reaction on my arm. I promised myself that I would only return to the power dynamics of television when I had a career built outside of it, in theater and cinema, because I would never go through that again. So, I immersed myself in the theater every day of the week, taught classes to teenagers, and did commercials.

Theater kept me working every day of the week. On Mondays and Tuesdays, I did stand-up comedy; on Wednesdays and Thursdays, I did a play in an alternate time slot; and on the weekends, primetime plays. I was earning my place in professional theater in Rio and São Paulo. I was a working actress. However, I didn't have a voice. The Philosophy course sustained my soul, questing my thirst for knowledge, but I was still not capable of "filling my own cup." I had not yet found my own voice.

I continued to work and learn a great deal until, one day, my "own cup" started to fill. The need for a certain story led me to produce myself in a play. Since then, I have been compelled to acquire a basic understanding of business management and self-management, as I would have to take the reins of my plays as well as my professional route.

I was 19 years old and had a great mentor, Camila Amado, who told me: if you want to have a free, autonomous, and authentic artistic life, start being your own producer. And that's what I did. In addition to taking acting classes with Camila, I organized her library with all the major classics of world drama. I read everything you can imagine: from Nordic to Spanish playwrights. At a young age, I was already performing in plays written by Garcia Lorca, Ibsen, and Shakespeare. All of this experience gave me a solid foundation for my artistic life.

As you'll discover in this book, I am intense. Not satisfied with just diving into world drama, I would intertwine it with philosophy, which I was already delving into in college. Yet, I'd still rock my plastic sandals and denim shorts like a true Carioca, a *girl from Ipanema*.

Although we may come across as carefree, our minds are filled with a wealth of culture.

Now, let's unravel how you're going to become an UNLEASHED woman.

PART 2

BECOMING UNLEASHED

The transformative journey towards being unleashed is a teaching method to prepare women to become the entrepreneurs and protagonists of their own lives, regardless of age, origin, color, race, beliefs, or financial background. The foundation is based upon the conviction that every woman has inside her the seed needed to grow her inner power. She can bring out her natural talents using the ability to believe in her own competence.

This "natural talent" is what you do best. In fact, it can be monetized and used to pay your bills, manage your business plan like a life project, and cultivate healthy relationships. You can adjust any wrong turns your life may have taken. The "Unleashed" Foundation speeds up this process with a number of actions that I have split into five major steps to make them easier to understand:

1. Developing resilience
2. Building independence
3. Sense of belonging
4. Leadership
5. What have I learned?
6. What's my legacy?

I will illustrate each step in this book based on my personal experiences. I assure you that it will be a simple and fluid process. When you least expect it, you will be a changed woman who appreciates herself even more.

TO START: Vulnerability is not bad quality. On the contrary, the more we get to know that side of ourselves, the better our chances of dealing with all that diminish our strengths and sabotage us. This way, we understand who we are and can defeat the inner villain that tries to undermine us.

Who is your inner villain? It is that voice whispering in your ear that you are incapable of making your dreams come true. Do you recognize it? Great. From now on, it is crucial that you identify and mute it. This may not be easy to do, but with proper nurturing, empathetic listening, and my guidance supporting you every step of the way, you will not be alone. Soon you will laugh at your inner villain, ordering them to bother someone else.

Why can I say that I understand you? Because I have my own inner villain, I have also doubted and sabotaged myself for not knowing my vulnerabilities. I have been where you are now. Our stories may differ, but I'm sure we all have had to face the capitalist patriarchy. It is based on the exclusion of women from the job market and their subordination to men, who have largely been in charge of the world since the 15th century when capitalism started to take shape.

The Caribbean-American, black, lesbian-feminist author Audre Lorde alerted, "One cannot destroy the master's house using the master's tools. Our challenge is to create different tools". I believe that each woman needs to find her own pace, starting with self-knowledge and a full understanding of her capabilities, body, and hormones. Hormones? Yes, my dear, differently from men, we are a deep well full of turbulent waters - it is biological. We feel and cry more, have stronger intuition, and cannot avoid that. As a result, we should not want to be like men. Since they were the ones who built the playground, we will always lose. We need to create our own professional amusement parks and make a ton of our own money.

For instance, we cannot simply pull up a random business plan from the internet. It fails to consider that we suffer from endometriosis, have terrible menstrual cramps, and may be unable to think straight one or two days a month. It's even worse if we are forced to juggle our professional lives with family life - partner, children, housework, school, playdates, and so on.

We know that taking on too much is still a reality for many women, especially Latinas. Let's be honest: how could we possibly plan our lives based on a professional PLAIN written by someone with none of those concerns? Do you see the problem here? That sets us up for failure. However, if we create our own business plan, which I call a life project, we start preparing our own ground for success.

I do not doubt that the best way to secure our own space is by forging alliances with other women. Since being founded, the "Dona de Si" (Unleashed) Institute in Brazil has promoted this female union through our groups on WhatsApp, Telegram, and where we celebrate our victories and partnerships and share our disappointments and good pieces of advice. In addition to social media, we have the institute's platform: the "DONA DE SI" (Unleashed) TRANSFORMATIVE JOURNEY has already helped more than two thousand women who have doubled their income by adjusting their self-management, embraced innovation, and monetizing ideas from the heart.

We do not believe in the phrase: "There is no money in that." We believe that anything can make money as long as it is properly planned, executed, and managed. No more of the limitations imposed upon us Latinas for centuries, even by the people we love. There is no dream that cannot cut a profit. Got it?

Since its beginning as an online column in a major fashion magazine in Brazil, "DONA DE SI" (Unleashed) has directly impacted over 500 thousand women. If we consider the heightened effect of social media, that number has surely exceeded 10 million. During this time, I established a common vocabulary with those women and enforced the notion that we have a wide range of skills that should be developed.

As for the students on our platform, who were on this journey for months through our master classes or our mentoring programs, we have seen them quickly flip the switch. Many of them started increasing their income, ending abusive relationships, and began believing in their own authenticity. Today, our positive rate of successful women in business makes this one of the most effective methods to equip them to live fuller lives. I am happy to say you can also become UNLEASHED, one step at a time.

STEP 1 – DEVELOPING RESILIENCE

The first challenge you face when setting out on the journey to becoming UNLEASHED is acting consciously. Let me tell you my own experience. When a friend (the Brazilian actress Maria Maya) and I decided to produce a play called "On the other side of the Afternoon," based on two stories by the renowned Brazilian writer Caio Fernando Abreu, it was not an easy task. We were super young (in our 20s) and made mistakes for lack of consciousness. Everything was going well until a certain point, but we soon realized we were on the wrong path. And, to make things right again, we were forced to change the airplane's fuel mid-flight.

ACT with awareness

Let me tell you what happened:

Since we had the will but not the money to put on the play, we contacted the person who managed the cultural space "Casa da Gávea" in Rio de Janeiro, a place we believed to be the appropriate size and style for our play, and said: "We don't have the money now, but we are very confident that we will bring in the audience and sell a lot of tickets. Are you in?"

They were in, so we negotiated with each professional involved, which ultimately allowed the play to come to life. In other words, the show was a collective effort. Everyone would be paid out of the ticket sales, and the money to pay for the light and sound equipment rental would also come from there. The little money we had – our meager savings – we invested in the set, costumes, and publicity photos.

The opening night was packed (with special guests) and received wide press coverage. However, on the second day, we were faced with a harsh reality: we sold only two tickets. Yes, two tickets! – which were probably bought by my parents. We didn't even cover the rental cost, and the result was that with each passing day, our debt increased.

We conducted ourselves with the consciousness of beginners who want to bring their dreams to life but only rely on great luck. Is that wrong? YES. Do many people make that mistake? YES. Do many people give up after that? YES. But you do not have to go through all that. You need to ACT CONSCIOUSLY.

Remember to make a financial provision for the bad days. You need a well-rounded marketing plan, which is as important as the financial part. That was another mistake we made. We believed all audiences would well receive the play, but that was not the case. An author like Caio Fernando Abreu, under the direction of Gilberto Gawronski, could never be a mass entertainment product. We were producing a very niche artistic play, which would only be appreciated by a select audience. We forgot to consider that when promoting it. Our focus was too broad, while our product was too specific.

You don't have to be a marketing genius. If you know your niche and where your public is and promote your product with that focus in mind, you will dramatically increase your chances of covering the bills to fulfill your dream. Today, social media helps a lot with that.

In 1998, that tool was not available to us, much less the notion that knowing each product's audience/client relationship is crucial. So, without marketing and a financial reserve, we failed to make money needed to honor our commitment to the theater management, the lighting and sound technicians, and the equipment rentals needed for the play.

That took a big emotional toll on us.

FEELINGS: how to keep it together

The feeling was akin to slamming into a wall at 100 km/h. It was a big reality shock, and I'm sure that happens to many female entrepreneurs. It is normal for a first business to fail in the business world. But I am here to help you skip that part. No, you do not need to go through that much disappointment to learn how to build your business. I am against romanticizing failure as if it dignifies the entrepreneur. Oh, please! Let's take a shortcut, shall we? No one who is UNLEASHED can afford to lose time with avoidable mistakes.

Tunica's (Maria Maya's nickname) and my mistake were avoidable, but we decided to face it since we failed to avoid it. I looked at the debts candidly, entered them into my accounting book, negotiated the terms to settle them, and went to work. Before I realized it, I was making exercise bike commercials on TV sales channels and even advertising pain medicine dressed in the medication packaging in order to settle the debts with my creditors. During that series of mistakes, we made some good choices: we kept the play going, did not make new debts, and, most importantly, sat down and talked about it all.

We went to a convenience store at a gas station, bought two beers, and took responsibility. It was one of the most beautiful moments I have ever shared with a business partner. We did not try to escape the blame. We were honest and, right there, seated on the sidewalk, feeling defeated, we had the idea that could ultimately save our project. We decided to submit our play to a number of theater festivals, which, at the time, were being held in several Brazilian cities.

That was our product niche. Those were the events where the audiences well-received cult plays, we were well paid, and our credibility increased. And: bam! We were right. The week after we submitted the play, we got three invitations from some of the biggest festivals in the country. So, with the fees we were paid, we settled our debts and even got back what we had invested. Phew!

I want you to be mindful of a few things: we were very young and naive artists. That is: it was the perfect recipe for a big fight between us, with one tossing blame toward the other. But we subverted the conventional logic and GOT A HANDLE ON OUR EMOTIONS. We acted as partners and were able to let the businesswoman prevail over the artist and found a solution. To this day, I am so very proud of our powerful, beer-infused insight.

At times like this, partnerships end, poorly made agreements come to light, and a lack of consistency becomes apparent. Don't let that happen, dearest UNLEASHED. If your partner freaks out when faced with adversity, do not allow their emotions to drag you into the mud of carelessness, putting everything on the line. You are taking the time to read this book, so in terms of maturity, you are already ahead of the women who have yet to read it.

Getting back up after the first professional fall is the impulse needed to take you farther. Do not avoid the responsibility of proposing solutions, getting a handle on your emotions, keeping calm, and learning to start over. Do not blame others for a problem that you created. Be accountable. Examine it. Work it out.

> **END the cycle**

Tunica and I decided to go ahead with the play. We presented at the festivals and visited cities with theaters with the right profile for our product. During that time, when we took the bull of failure by the horns, we also had lots of adventures: we met foreign artists, learned new theatrical languages, fell into traps set by shady local producers, and were successful in working with professional and serious ones.

In one of those cities, Porto Alegre, I believe, Tunica and I had another conversation that determined our next steps: we paused everything to understand what we had done up to that point, our individual career goals, and what we expected to achieve with the play. Today, I would call that pause "expectations alignment." A crucial starting point for any partnership. And once again, we refueled the plane mid-flight.

In another honest talk, we understood that we had similar goals: we produced the play so the establishment could see us. She did it so she would be more than just the daughter of two major Brazilian drama directors. I did it to be an actress who produces her own work. At that point, we had been involved with the play for two years, and our goals were being met. So, we managed to end the cycle of that play with three big accomplishments:

1. All our debts were settled. We evened out and neither made a profit nor had any lingering debts. We reinvested what we made in the tour;
2. We exercised our female partnership muscle;
3. We made a name for ourselves in the Brazilian arts, and proof of that was the amazing job invitations we got.

So, we decided it was time to "put the set away," pause the play and end that chapter of our lives. Naturally, at the time, I lacked the consciousness to assess how mature we were in dealing with our frustrations and getting a handle on our emotions. We had won, and there I understood that it is up to us to set the course, with the financial possibilities and the emotional awareness we have at the moment. And that the most important thing is to evolve. To move forward, we needed to end and honor that cycle. I understood that evolving does not mean never making another mistake again but improving how we fail so we don't hit head first. To this day, Tunica and I have unconditional love and admiration for each other due to the lessons we learned and the maturity we developed together.

EXPERIENCE

After that, I produced a play that brought me some "hard lessons," as it was my first production with a large sponsorship. In this experience, I made several mistakes with people management, but I also learned a great deal about crisis management.

I'll start at the beginning. I still lacked the security and self-confidence to sign a play, so I asked a friend, who was already a professional playwriter, to write a play based on one of the books of Simone de Beauvoir. I wanted to talk about the pressure of marriage in a woman's life, and Simone introduced ideas and raised questions that were wildly appropriate.

I commissioned the work around 2001, but the production only came out in 2004 because I couldn't do it without sponsorship money. I wanted to take a bigger step in terms of quality and management. So, I opened my own production company and began the quest of fundraising under the Brazilian Rouanet Act.

The Rouanet Act is a certificate issued by the Ministry of Culture of Brazil for your project, following a detailed examination of the budget and all of the production company's documents in order to secure funding from corporate tax exemptions. The funding authorization process is lengthy, and it is even more difficult to find a company that believes in the project and is willing to invest in your art part of the income tax that would otherwise be paid to the government.

In 2004, I finally secured an investment with a company engaged in the hotel business: they would deposit the sponsorship money in the project's account – tied to the Brazilian Ministry of Culture – and I would have to spend exactly what was stated in the original budget. Any other costs had to be explained, which is absolutely fair. After all, it is public money and must be managed responsibly.

The first payment I made was to the writer I hired. We signed a contract that stipulated a delivery date and established that I could make changes to the material if necessary. Besides, together we chose the director and the cast that would perform in the play. When we started rehearsing, I was overcome with such joy that all I cared about was the play, the characters, and every artistic aspect, while my production partner handled payments, contracts, and so on. However, I forgot to include people management in this management equation.

We decided to do some exercises on the matter. With the writer present during rehearsals, she was able to write based on our improvisations, which she loved doing. I put all my energy into this and failed to notice the increasing animosity between the director and the writer. When I did realize it, it was too late: they could no longer be in the same place without getting into a heated argument.

When I took on the role of serving leader, I failed to set limits. This free work style puts the director in the position of "boss." By taking over that space, she started feeling more important than the author, who, in turn, felt vulnerable and uncomfortable in her writing assignment. As a result, the writer did not deliver the entire play in time for opening night, which put huge stress on the team. The director used scenes we had improvised to finish the play. It was horrible. I couldn't believe I worked that hard to have such a messy production as a result.

I was forced to accept that new reality because I had contracts with the theater, the sponsor, the media company, and everyone else involved that did not allow for a postponement without a penalty - there was no money left for that. The play opened in Rio, and the playwriter only delivered the final product two weeks later, but by then, we couldn't change anything. Her resentment turned to me, the producer, the leader, the one person who had done what everyone had asked. She demanded that her play be entirely staged, but we could not pause the showings. I had no idea how to solve that.

So I stopped, thought about it, made a list of priorities, problems, and solutions (which is why I insist that lists are the best way to get back on track), and found that: 1) the product delivered by the writer, albeit late, was the reason behind all my work, so it had to be used; 2) the director was not acting professionally, she was disrespecting the writer and myself, displaying a childish behavior that ultimately made her involvement in the project impossible.

It was time for me to learn that serving also means setting boundaries. It was up to me, the dreamer of the project, to get a hold of that runaway train putting it back on the tracks. Consequently, I made the following decisions: I ended the play's run in Rio de Janeiro earlier than expected, set aside a portion of the funds I would have spent on media services, and changed the play using the writer's whole text.

As a result, I finally opened in São Paulo the complete play I had worked so hard to produce. I kept the cast, and the direction was taken over by one of the actresses under my supervision. We used the whole play, which was the goal in the first place, and the show was a huge success! We ran from Wednesday through Sunday, with a full house every single day.

Interestingly, between unconscious and conscious leadership with set boundaries, I found that the latter avoids personal crises the most. In addition, it's best suited to any form of management. When I started serving the written text and setting boundaries for the ideas incompatible with the writer's ideas and mine, I faced another kind of problem: the bruised ego – which is much easier to deal with than the inflated ego.

At the end of the run, I did not take the play on tour because my energy was drained. But the feelings of accomplishment and the success story of a dream come true were right there inside me. Along with the results of excellent financial management: with the budget for one play, I produced two. How did I do it? By establishing a partnership with media services, which is always the most expensive part. Whew! The whirlwind was over, and I had learned a lesson that I have since applied throughout my professional career: NEVER PRETEND YOU DON'T SEE THE PERSONAL CONFLICTS WITHIN YOUR TEAM.

At first sight, it might seem exhausting to manage people individually. Within a group, a team, it seems excruciating. But it is not. After that dramatic episode, I started to enjoy working with people and scanning each professional individually, even before hiring them. Understanding the strengths and weaknesses of each person avoids crises. And remember: a crisis is NEVER managed by machines but rather by the people operating the machines. So, managing crises means managing vulnerabilities, insecurities, and projections.

This production was a big learning opportunity for me. After putting the set away in the warehouse, I did another assessment, this time from outside the crisis. I looked at it from a distance and decided that:

1. I would never have a partnership. I am a leader;
2. I would always make the roles and responsibilities of each team member very clear and well-established beforehand;
3. If anyone consistently refused to understand their roles and responsibilities, there would be no argument: the person would be fired.

Just like that, I shifted from being a manager who fantasized about her work and became a manager with a more professional perspective, less driven by "friendships." From then on, I would make each project even more purposeful and pleasurable at the same time. I can safely say that I have never made that mistake again. And again, I needed to honor that cycle in order to move forward.

TO UPHOLD and press on

When I talk about honoring my mistakes, I mean honoring everything, the good and the bad. One cannot be UNLEASHED without owning the whole process. That is what will ensure their professional credibility.

Note: don't believe that a story of artistic entrepreneurship is different from any other. It can be the college class you teach, the earrings you make, or the exam you plan to take. For any path you design, you will have to be the manager of your own life, an UNLEASHED, and each no you say to set a boundary is a yes to the proper management of your project.

TO BE UNLEASHED means to embrace and fully experience it all.

To end this Step 1, I have one final tip I know might not be easy: find a way to honor the entire path you traveled, either by writing about it or by giving yourself time to process everything you experienced, but do it. My trick is to make lists, and I suggest you start there. It is a good exercise to get to know yourself better. List your victories and your defeats, and never blame someone else. If you're the leader, the responsibility is entirely yours. Take charge for the full experience and explore the new strength that resides within you, which you must awaken: the strength of accountability, the strength of someone who will not be victimized.

Women have a historical DNA – often more relevant than the biological one – that requires us to be constantly in action, overburdened, and exhausted. It makes us forget to validate our past experiences, both positive and negative. Especially our positive experiences. That is self-sabotage. Be mindful of how you organize your time, of your unknowing "obligation" to be the well-behaved family girl. Enough is enough, right? The well-behaved girl might not build anything worthwhile. To that end, you'd be well served by browsing the biographies of Mother Theresa of Calcutta or Sister Maura Clark. Even actual SAINTS can be, each in their own manner, UNLEASHED women.

STEP 2 – BUILDING INDEPENDENCE (PAYING YOUR BILLS)

This step is about that moment in your life or in your business when you say: "I have made plenty of mistakes and learned a lot, and now I can build something that's going to work and give me the financial independence that I have craved. It's time to put myself to the test".

There is a lovely term for this: entrepreneurship. It is widely disseminated in the corporate world and is often used to reference the incorporation of new businesses or, for companies that are already established, it is usually associated with change and risks. I have always understood entrepreneurship as a way of acting in life: in terms of what I identify with and want to do, what I want to achieve, and the goal that motivates me.

> **YOU ARE your own enterprise**

The feeling you get when thinking of yourself as UNLEASHED, who holds the reins of her life decisions, is amazing. There is no denying it. But I must alert you: the only purpose of that is, primarily, to pay the bills. However, the good thing about it is that the more capable you become of paying your bills, the closer you get to being a free woman who owns her thoughts and, especially, takes responsibility for her own choices. No matter who agrees with them. This is not a romantic notion but rather a joyful reality.

> # YOUR BILLS
> ## will drive you

From the moment you're able to pay all your bills, your professional life will be under your control. So, in this step, your focus has to be on paying your bills at the end of the month. Only that will allow you to stop being a woman who procrastinates, who has many ideas but never follows through on any of them, or even a woman who criticizes other independent women. Paying your bills will remove you from the role of VILLAIN of your own life.

As with all the choices we make in life, this has advantages and disadvantages. Remember: you chose to be UNLEASHED. Prepare yourself because when you're buried in debt, the only way to start building your professional independence – unless you were born rich – is a lot of people will whisper in your ear that you're crazy for taking such a big risk. And the worst part is that when the credit card bill arrives, and you can't pay the full amount, you will find yourself agreeing with them, feeling inclined to walk by them with your head low, thinking: "They warned me and, despite that, I insisted and screwed up."

On the other hand, even if you make the money to honor your commitments, you are likely to mess up when the money starts coming in. That is because you – like most women – did not receive financial education in school, and much less from your family. Don't beat yourself up!

Little by little, you will become your money's best friend and learn to become more organized with it, separating your personal expenses from your business costs. You will learn how to save and make it grow until the time comes when you will be able to look straight at those people who called you "crazy" and say: "Things are like this because it is my business, and now I know how to manage my wealth." That's right, whether it is a little or a lot of money, you will be generating wealth and abundance, adding to the chain that sustains the world's economy.

> **DEAR BOSS,**
> **I need a raise**
> **because I'm drowning**
> **in debt**

But, in order for that to happen, you must stand up and face the battles that make up your journey. This is when you must understand the difference between shame and necessity. Here lie the crucial crossroads where you will be forced to choose your path: either crawl back into your room and hide, ashamed for not feeling up to the fight, making millions of excuses for yourself, and thus allowing yourself to remain disconnected from the world; or you step out of that place, driven by the need to pay your bills and the desire to achieve your goals and everything else that will make your path enjoyable and appealing. So, beautiful: what is it going to be?

Believe me: the obligation of paying your water and electrical bills, your groceries, and your rent is good and powerful. It protects you from abusive relationships and domestic violence and affords you spiritual growth and full-blown happiness. It also leads you to your next step: YOUR BUSINESS HAS TAKEN OFF!

UP CLOSE SHE ain't NORMAL!

This play was not just something that I wrote and staged. It was a statement of my belief in life that came from my soul's depths. It was raw. Perhaps, the biggest exposure I have ever subjected myself to since it did not show a strong, determined Suzi, someone I have often attempted to personify. It showcased an insecure Suzi who was not quite clear about how to build her own path. It portrayed a loser personality; a woman convinced that everything she touched ultimately went wrong: the alter ego of the entrepreneur of her own life, putting all her vulnerabilities on display. I believe the focus I chose for the text, which came so naturally and from the heart, was, in fact, what caused the audience to connect so strongly with the play, allowing it to withstand for fifteen years and to multiply into various content: a web series at GSHOW and the comedy franchise of UP CLOSE, SHE AIN'T NORMAL, one of the most profitable in Brazil.

When I decided to produce Up Close She ain't Normal! I was at a point in my life where I had already graduated from college and produced a number of plays in order to have work. But I had not yet found my own voice. I was just one of many. After graduation, I felt safe enough to introduce myself as an author because that is the most important thing I learned from Aristotle, the Greek philosopher. Because of my previous work, I got into the market and became a working actress who works regularly. With an appearance here, and a play there, I was working a lot, but I had not stated my purpose yet. I had not shown what I was capable of doing.

My feeling was that I lacked a signature in my career, my own artistic stamp. So, I decided it was time to show myself as an actress, an author, and a producer. Note: putting a signature on your work is important in all professions. A signature is to say: how I do it, this is what I believe, and this is what distinguishes my product from the others. It was time, I'm not sure if it was the right time, but I had to show courage, to go all the way in. After all, I had studied hard and had a bunch of bills to pay. I thought: now,

I will take my chance. I wrote Up Close She Is Not Normal! in just one week.

But hold on. It wasn't like: I was in the shower, and, all of a sudden, I had a genius idea, and all the words overflooded my head. No. I had been preparing for that. I had already outlined the framework of the play and had been jotting down ideas in a little notebook for some time. That week, I isolated myself at home, disconnected from the world, and wrote a story about a woman who wanted to make it but had no idea how to do it. She attempts a number of different paths that other people have said to be the "right" ones. In each one, she fails in a different and funny way. Until she finally reconnects with her inner child and does everything according to that little girl's belief system. From that point on, the protagonist's life works out, and she makes it.

When I finished writing the play, I did not think twice: I took the money I had in a savings account – you know, that cash you set aside to take a vacation with your friends to an awesome beach? – and invested it in the pre-production of the play. It was three thousand *reais*, about a thousand dollars back then. A negligible amount for a professional play, but I did it anyway.

The production was just me, a chair, and some clothes. No director and no crew. It all existed solely in my head. I staged the play at the theater schools where I used to teach. In a couple of months, I had gotten my investment back. I had not made a profit but recovered my investment and gained something priceless: confidence! I was confident in the quality of the entertainment product I had created, not to mention that I had managed to map out my target audience. Bingo! I was ready to take the next step and broaden my reach.

Being the producer, I conducted extensive research on all the writing contests and open calls at the time and entered the play in several of them. And guess what? I ended up winning one. It was a contest held by the Federal Bank of Brazil for new playwriters. It might not seem like a lot of money, only twenty-five thousand *reais* (about six thousand dollars), but to me, it was a fortune! I managed to hire a director, Flavio Garcia da Rocha; an art director, Ellen Milet, who is super smart and generous; a sound and lighting technician; and two production assistants. That's how I began phase two of the journey of my play Up Close She ain't Normal!

It was a huge success. On the second day, I had to do an extra show. On the third, my father had to help out at the ticket counter because there were scalpers selling tickets, and the police had to be called. Total madness! It's like I was selling a cake and, all of a sudden, everyone said at once: "I want to buy it, now!"

To this day, I cannot explain how all the shows were sold out since opening night. Actually, yes, I can. A lot of things contributed to the play's success: it was staged in a theater in downtown Rio de Janeiro, on a Wednesday, at seven in the evening. People left work and went to the theater instead of facing rush hour traffic.

I mean, I did not do the play inside of a theater, but at a bar, on tables, which we would cover with a red carpet (leftover from another play) for me to walk on. The stage consisted of a few tables that we put together, bringing a little more charm to the audience's happy hour. There was a separate space with a few chairs for those who just wanted to watch the play without eating or drinking. The strategy was to draw the attention of the people at the bar to the play and then add the ticket price to their tabs.

I thought about the whole marketing strategy, even the photo on the banner, where I flashed a big smile alongside the title of the play to entice the audience. In week two, the management of "Caixa Cultural" (the Federal Bank Cultural Agency) booked the play to perform at several of its units around the country. I secured a paid tour, performing in Rio, Salvador, Brasília, São Paulo, and Curitiba. In each city, the audience came, I thanked them and paid the crew and my personal bills.

That is why I urge you: wherever you are, do not stay hidden as you attempt to market your product. Always be closing. Go online. Put yourself out there. Go everywhere. Own what you do. Find out where your audience is, research it, draw up a strategy, and sell your product or service. This way, the success that comes from your intelligence will gift you something priceless: the personal strength to find your voice.

> **EMPOWERMENT to find your voice**

I am so sure about this because it was only when I started to own what I was doing that I finally understood I possessed a personal strength that gave me my own voice. Please note that I am telling you this to ensure that you, too, find the seedling of your personal strength and discover that your voice can impact your market niche.

We all have that strength, and our journey is about expressing it. Now, remember one thing: our personal strength does not come from nothing. It materializes during the process of becoming UNLEASHED, seamlessly. If you overthink, you might feel paralyzed and give up. Remember that your strength comes from doing. Once you find it (which involves knowing your vulnerability), you become the protagonist of your story.

PROTAGONISM

With the success of Up Close She ain't Normal! I understood the meaning of the word protagonist. It had nothing to do with looking powerful in a picture, wearing high heels, or using makeup. Protagonism comes from a Greek word: Prota = first, and Agon = battlefield. The protagonist is the first to enter the battlefield, the person who will take the first hit, and the first trophy. They are the ones who actively protect their family, their team, their peers, and everyone else who is by their side during the journey. It is the person who has the attitude and the voice that makes themselves get there first. That is what makes them leaders and protagonists.

However, it is worth noting that not everyone who is UNLEASHED will be the leader of everything, but they will always be the leader of their own life. Do you get that? This book does not propose to make you a leader at all costs. You will be your life's leader, which is the biggest achievement of the new century.

Don't think that once you become the protagonist of your life, your work will be done. Not at all! Leadership is a new muscle to the female psyche, and, therefore, it requires daily exercise, assessments, and adjustments. The muscle of female protagonism that is in all of us must be trained often. It is different with men, as they are raised to hold that position in the world. We are not, and it takes more effort on our part. We must also be careful to develop our protagonism in our own way, considering our emotions, intuitions, and peculiarities: feminine stuff. Never, ever, should you attempt to lead like a man.

Expressions such as "she proved that she has some big balls," "she is as fierce as a man," and "she is so good you forget she's a woman" need to be wiped out of the marketplace. Meanwhile, it is up to you to reject and correct anyone who uses them, replying that you are "the best because you're a woman." Got it?

GOALS

Building independence means exercising protagonism, which can also mean bringing in financial stability. By being proactive and exercising protagonism, we can make great strides toward success. If the play's performances were consistently packed, I could pay my bills and crew and even save some money for myself.

From that point on, I started setting goals for that money and strategizing ways to multiply it. In December of 2006, I was at a restaurant in Rio with my crew, and I said, "Mark my words: in 2011, I will be in the biggest concert hall in Rio de Janeiro showing Up Close She Is Not Normal! and it will be packed. Make a note of this and hold on to it!" I love doing that because I am also committing the crew to my goal and throwing my intention out into the universe. My plan was to put three thousand people into a concert hall within five years. And the big question was: how could I build the path to get there?

I knew one thing: I needed to set aside a portion of the money that was coming in to be reinvested in the play. So, I used the three-envelope technique. If you are like me and have a hard time balancing your accounts, and just looking at a spreadsheet makes you dizzy, the envelopes can be a big help.

Back then, I didn't have any help managing the play, and the theater did not take credit card payments. It was cash only. And so, I used three envelopes: in one of them, I put my payment per show; in the second, the payments I had to make; and in the third, the amount to be reinvested toward play. My money went into my personal account, the crew's went into each person's account, and the reinvestment I deposited into my production company's account. That's how I organized myself and did five tours in Brazil without any new sponsorship, other than the new playwriter's contest I mentioned earlier. Since it was a monologue, I traveled with a technician and a producer. Everything was thought out to ensure minimal cost with the best possible quality, making sure that the ticket sales would fill all the envelopes."

During the first year of the play, something unexpected happened, even though I had that set as a goal: the market began to see me as a professional actress and writer. Many television and movie directors and casting executives went to see the play or sent their assistants. One day, while in my dressing room, I was invited to test for Elite Squad, a movie by director José Padilha. Following that, I was hired to work on the series *A Diarista and Minha Nada Mole Vida* (The housekeeper of my not-so-easy life) and as a screenwriter for the production company Conspiração Filmes.

Suddenly, several investors found out about my business and decided to invest in it. Before I knew it, I was working on telenovelas and movies, doing gigs here and there while still touring with my play. My life was crazy. I would look at everything that was going on and think: "Wow, I had chosen the right strategy to be seen just as I wanted!" I transitioned from working only as an actress to being both an actress and an author who earned more respect within the market. This recognition and the invitations came in, and I showcased the high quality of my work.

Alongside that success, I had to confront unjust market practices targeting women. I'm talking about the questions we're frequently compelled to answer, the misogyny underlying them, and the disrespect they entail. My success is always called to question: "Who is this woman who writes, produces, and acts? Doesn't she think a bit too much of herself?" Or: "Who is this woman anyway to think she can be a big-time chef?" and "How about that other one who wants to take the examination to be a judge?"

Have no doubt: the market (whichever it is) will put you down. After all, we are the intruders in the professional scenario fabricated by men. We are oppressed daily, albeit subtly, like soft clouds passing by distractedly – and, sometimes, rudely even – to make us give up and go back to "our place" as assistants to the bigshot male protagonists.

In Latin America, we live in a macho culture (I believe the same happens here in North America): if a woman has a nice ass, she can't have brains. And if you're Brazilian, there's no way out of it. We have curvy bodies, period. Should we be reduced to mere objects? Of course not. I can't tell you how many times I was the only woman in my writing groups and heard people say: "I didn't think the Suzana Pires writer was also the actress." Why not? Can't a woman write? Should we not be allowed to multitask? Can't we make more money than you, idiot? There was a time I used to be the Queen of the Quips because that was the shield I developed to survive among the sharks that insisted on tossing me out of the industry.

Dear reader, don't think I understood this game right from the start. No! I suffered a great deal and did everything I could to be taken seriously: I went to meetings wearing clothes that did not reveal my body, spoke in a very serious tone, and did not giggle at anyone. Until I realized I was frozen, distant from my soul. I decided to act like myself at creative meetings. I started to laugh like myself, to tell my misogynistic colleague to be quiet when I was speaking, and, every now and then, I would wear a tight outfit and very high heels so that they would feel uncomfortable in my presence.

These boys are so afraid of the female intensity. But I was playing to win and was not about to drown in the writing room. I was talented and delivered everything on time, according to the budget. I did not allow myself to make mistakes. I always got it right. Naturally, all the pressure amounted to a steep cost in therapy sessions. But they did not debilitate me, and I survived my first years as the protagonist of my life in that misogynist industry.

Back then, I wrote a show about sex for a cable TV channel and was performing in two very successful plays in São Paulo: Toalete, by Walcyr Carrasco, and Up Close She Ain't Normal! It was very unlikely that I would fail. But, to manage everything I had going on, I had to adopt a strict routine for my life: work, work, work, very few parties, and several failed relationships. What could I do if my partners couldn't support and admire my battles? It was their loss.

As you can see, the journey to becoming UNLEASHED is permeated with the infamous unconscious misogynist bias, which everyone has, even us. During the step of building independence, most women experience the impostor syndrome, which is when you are starting to achieve your goals but haven't realized it yet. That's when we start doubting our own capabilities. Then we look around seeking reassurance but find no female references in our professional field. Or, when they exist, they are way above or way under you. You feel lonely and start to believe that you will have to do it all alone and end up overburdening yourself. The result? Bankruptcy.

That is the female situation in the job market worldwide. We must be aware of this and not label ourselves as victims because this will continue to be the situation for many women for a long time. We need to not partake in self-sabotage but actually understand our worth and consciously move ahead.

In my case, after the first three years of performing Up Close She Ain't Normal! on a crazy schedule, overseeing the whole production, writing for a major production company, and working as an actress, I realized that if I went on like that, my health would soon give in. Emotionally, I could not go on for another year that way. I decided to call in a producer to take over the play. I hired a junior producer to take care of the bureaucratic stuff. This was an investment I made in my business, so the overwork didn't bring me down.

In your case, it could be that moment when you have to recruit an intern to help manage your company because you have started mixing up your company's and your personal accounts. Take action to avoid your battle as a PROTAGONIST becoming exhausting. It is important to have a team, even if it is minimal, to help you get on track, face reality, and have time left to adjust the course of your business. Only then you will begin to understand your purpose.

PURPOSE

The purpose is what fuels our desire to keep up the war on the battlefield, which is the construction of female freedom. It is what will determine new goals and prevent us from doing something crazy, like swearing at your disgusting boss or telling all those stupid idiots to go f$#% themselves. I'll give you an example: I was starting to appear on television with a very popular character and was still unfamiliar with the world of celebrity press. At times, I had the urge to give reporters a snarky answer, but I controlled myself so I wouldn't blow everything. And I would act the same way whenever a director would say something unpleasant.

My purpose was the only thing keeping my big mouth shut and forcing me to be patient. I would hear things and pretend I didn't, or I would simply laugh them off, never allowing myself to be incensed because I had a bigger picture in mind: that my career as an actress and my career as a writer would coexist and that was starting to happen. Anyway, I was taking the first steps towards unprecedented personal development, forcing me to take risks, face my fears, and reinforce my courage.

Now, I ask you: if you apply this example to your own product, does it make sense?

> **RISK**
> **FEAR**
> **COURAGE**

Taking risks is crucial for the courage to lead the way and for fear to turn into strategic planning, creating a solid foundation upon which to stand. That's the key to calculated risk: PLANNING.

You must bear in mind that your purpose is always bigger than your daily goals. A goal is what you use to move from one point to another. Your purpose is what fuels that journey. After you establish your motivation (it could change with every step) – whether it be to provide the best for your family, to make a product that improves people's lives, or to pay off your apartment, etc. – you will have to set a course for your next goals, which should be bigger than the goals you have already achieved, and that means taking risks.

Mind you, we are still on Step 2, which is crucial, as it assumes that you will have to take a risk, which could be financial, an extremely high emotional stake, or even learning a new technique to pursue a specialty. Now, you will have to take on bigger things: a larger team or a more important job. You will have to face the

BROKEN STEP, the one that only exists for minorities climbing toward power: everyone sees the same staircase and believes they can climb it, but one step is broken, and that is where women trip and fall. It's unconscious. Think about a time your boss gave a promotion to a less qualified guy, but he's a man, or when you were harassed. It's even worse when you hit the glass ceiling. What are those obstacles about?

They are a limitation that the market puts in our minds. That ceiling is translucent, like glass, thus its name. We slam our heads on it, look up, and see things happening where we want to be, but we cannot get there because it is stopping us. Do you know how that ceiling actually works? You know you are competent and have delivered the results to justify a promotion or a better contract, but then you realize that the prick at the next desk has passed you by. Has that ever happened to you? I am sure it did. Or it will. Sorry, but it is unavoidable.

I am not saying that you should accept that limitation. Of course not! But you must be aware of it and learn how to break through it without nobody's consent. When this time comes, we will have gotten through the first three years, started to invest more heavily in our business, and evaded bankruptcy. By then, we have been fighting the fight for about six or seven years, proving our worth every step of the way. It is time to take down that barrier, bring the wrecking ball to the glass and make some noise, shattering it so we can access the space we deserve.

Just don't forget that the ceiling is made of glass, so the woman who manages to break it risks getting hurt on its pieces. Believe me: that's how it goes. Some women get hurt badly, others less. But there is no escaping it. And what heals our wounds so that all we are left with are the scars? Purpose. That 'something bigger' will heal our open wounds. For the scars, on the other hand, I prescribe therapy. It is crucial.

Risk involves fear, which, in turn, requires courage. Fear is a must for courage to exist, but the latter must be greater, and it will be driven by purpose, which provides you with resilience.

I love this picture of me in front of a huge audience because it shows where courage has taken me. I had just taken the biggest leap of my career. I had reinvested in my play, filling Brazil's largest theaters. The year 2011 was in the past, and an audience of

3 thousand people watching the play was an ordinary occurrence. Additionally, I had left the big production company I used to work for and was the only woman to be hired as an actress and a writer by the third largest television company in the world.

I had already been there for a few years, working as a co-writer to an important writer. The glass ceiling was being appropriately broken, I was evolving daily. I took on greater responsibility and failed to realize the emotional toll that came along. That is why I felt the need to write this book: so you can go through it all easily.

It had been ten years since the play first opened. Now, it would migrate to a different medium with the release of the web series Look of the Day with Aunt Suelly, a spin-off debuting on the online platform of the company I worked for. There would be thirteen episodes, which I wrote with Alê Marson and Thiago Pasqualoto, the director was Alex Medeiros, and it was the biggest word-of-mouth experience on the platform at the time – the year was 2015.

It was my first experience with multimedia combining my two talents: acting and writing. I was ecstatic and realized I needed to learn more about how to combine those talents into a single product. I decided to study a new way of helming an entertainment product in Los Angeles: the job of the so-called showrunner, the mythical character that runs the show.

After twenty years in the business, I realized that my experience as an indie producer, an actress on a recording set, and a TV writer required some convergence of thought. Naturally, the Americans (who dominated the market) had already been training and exporting such professionals, like Tina Fey, Shonda Rhimes, and Ava DuVernay, just to name a few women. So, there I went.

While I was studying in the US, I found misogyny and oppression, but women here were better organized and active through organizations such as the Geena Davis Institute on Gender in Media and the #metoo. Such things are still in baby steps in countries like Brazil. In addition to mastering the art of combining my talents to work as a showrunner, I also caught the "female network bug."

I came back from that experience in the US straight to a number of performances of my play. I had finally reconnected with my inner child, the girl on the balcony who used to put on plays for relatives and neighbors at her grandparents' house in Brazil. She had come back to me with everything she had. I know this because a sense of freedom, the assurance that I was doing the best I could, and the conviction that life made sense, no matter how bad things got – feelings that only a child can genuinely have – took over me at that moment. And I was sure that I was on the right path.

It's funny that, when that happens, our eyes sparkle, and everyone assumes: "Are you in love?" And the answer is: "Yes, I am. I am in love with myself and everything I am building."

BUILDING A NEW IMAGE ON TOP OF MY WORK AS AN ACTRESS

At that point, I was an actress that performed in one soap opera after another and a writer who wrote soap operas and comedy shows. I was working sixteen to eighteen hours a day. I ultimately had to delegate the production of the play to a seasoned professional because I could no longer do it, not even with the help of the junior producer. I could hop on a plane and perform, but no more than that. That's when Leo Fuchs and Mauro Lemos became my partners in the play. We did another tour throughout Brazil and another run in Rio de Janeiro, which was a huge success.

Meanwhile, I took another step forward: I proposed to my television artist director to write a screenplay for a film based on my play. Guess what? It got the green light. There I started yet another multiplication of the 3 thousand reais (1 thousand dollars) I initially invested in the play. The budget for the movie was 10 million reais (3 million dollars). Right then, I closed the "Building independence" step, which begins with your bills and ends when you multiply your initial investment exponentially.

However, remember this is just one step, not the whole journey. Your management skills have to improve with each new Dollar that comes in. You cannot disconnect from everything the moment you start making a profit. The more money that comes in, the more careful you have to be with your finances. The time will come to build your egg nest, buy a house, and invest in your business. From now on, the most important thing is to refine your leadership skills and the sense of belonging for yourself and your team.

STEP 3 – HOW TO BUILD TEAMS AND MAKE IT WORK WITH DIVERSE PEOPLE

Now, I need to set the narrative back in time to talk about the element of BELONGING within my journey and its importance. I FELT VERY LONELY when I started taking the first steps toward being UNLEASHED. I had some friends but was not part of an inner circle. I didn't know anyone important that could offer me a hand and say: "Come on in, join us." On the one hand, if that caused me frustration because it made everything harder, it also stirred in me a feeling of not belonging *just yet*. Eventually, I would belong and have my own people and team.

What was my path toward belonging in the entertainment industry? Before I was an artist developing her voice, I was just a working actress in countless productions. At the time, I was building my reputation as an excellent professional, taking chances on things I had never done – like stand-up comedy and musicals – and showing the people who hired me how I worked. During that phase, I understood that the only thing I could have considered to be an "advantage" was my professionalism. It helped me to belong to a number of groups and to distinguish the reputable people in the market from the unreliable ones.

Yep, in the entertainment industry, especially at the beginning of your career, you meet many shady characters: delirious people who promise everything an artist dreams of but never see anything through and keep the naive artist's savings. That's the ugly truth. The only thing that protected me from that sort of people was my habit of demanding contracts, agreements in writing, and timeframes for the execution of goals. I was quick to identify a trap. After a while, I could see the problem even before all these steps and decided I would not belong to that crowd.

Belonging doesn't just happen; it shouldn't become a problem that lands on your lap. Anyone who is UNLEASHED uses what goes wrong to understand what will be good for them and help choose the group to which they belong.

Besides the unreliable types, I have also come across the unscrupulous but talented ones, which are harder to identify, but once you do, it becomes clear as day. These people will always be in your life since they are hired for their talent (and for their side dealings), but if you are prepared not to need to be everyone's friend, you will easily avoid them.

The big trap that the need to belong can represent for a woman who is building her own path lies precisely in the historical conditioning of our DNA to be obedient, pleasant, and nice to everyone. That leads us to believe that a mere expression of flattery is synonymous with friendship. We become an easy mark for unethical people. Until we reach the point where we have been so used, cheated, and jerked around we can no longer believe anything. We mope around, complaining that we're too trusting in people. Oh, please! I am saying this because I have been through that more times than I should have: DO NOT BE THE "NICE GIRL" AT WORK. BE PROFESSIONAL.

Whatever the field of work, each person is there to defend their little space of power, their stipend to pay the bills, and the praise to feed their unrestrained ego. Remember: the nice girl phase is O-V-E-R. Then you ask me: "But, Suzi, how am I going to do that? Didn't you tell me to put my heart into everything? I don't understand!" Let me explain, dear reader: you should put your heart into everything you do and get originality and higher pay in return. I did not say that you should put your heart into every person. The name of that is emotional insecurity, not belonging. Please don't be put off by how harshly I express this. My intention is to ensure that you will suffer less than I did, ok?

I was not a victim of anyone but myself when I mistook a team for a group of friends, or a coffee break for a gathering with cake at my grandmother's house, or even my cast for my family. All of that taught me valuable lessons, and the most important one was understanding the true meaning of BELONGING.

It means being one of the links in a production chain and nothing more. You can be the main link, which sets the tone and the cadence for the other links, the last or the middle link. But every one of them has a purpose within their production chain. That's all. Nothing more. If you identify with someone within that production chain to the point that the person becomes a friend, you should know exactly what you're doing so you won't regret it later, ok? I insist: what will protect you is your level of professionalism.

Showing PROFESSIONALISM does not mean acting like an emotionless robot. It means establishing your role within the production chain and determining your compensation (salary, fee, etc.). After everything is arranged, it means throwing yourself into the work and doing the best you can within the scope of your assignment. Acting professionally means delivering excellent quality rather than personal dilemmas.

Even though I learned early on how to be extremely professional, emotional insecurity has always been a problem for me, and I am sure it also has for you. When I was one of the links in the production chain, it was easier to deal with this: being knocked down straight on and learning the hard way not to be an idiot and to speak the language of the market. When I became the main link, the leader, it grew even harder to set aside my personal feelings and focus on belonging – I'll talk about this later in this book. For now, let's stay the course at the beginning of the process of belonging in your own field of work. You need someone you admire to treat you like a colleague; that is one of the clearest signs that you belong to that world where you have fought so hard to be.

SENSE OF BELONGING

I had my first real feeling of belonging on the day that Fernanda Montenegro (a famous Brazilian actress) ran into me and stopped to say hello. I thought: "Wow! I can't believe this. The one and only Brazilian actress icon knows who I am, has seen my work, and acknowledges me as a colleague. Now can I say I belong in this industry, right?"

The next time was when I acted opposite Laura Cardoso, who treated me as a real colleague. And, later on, when I wrote for her in two soap operas. We talked about the characters, made decisions together, and exchanged opinions about the best ways to go. That woman from whom I had learned so much actually listened to what I had to say. Right there, I knew I belonged.

You, who are UNLEASHED, are urged to stop and think: who are the people in your field who would represent the same thing to you? If you were a doctor, who would you say this about: "Wow, I was in the same room with doctor so-and-so!?" Or, if you're a stylist: "My Gosh, I'm here talking to whatshername, who's considered the biggest fashion designer in the world, and she likes my work!?" Or, even if you are in the food business: "Chef so-and-so said that I'm good!" When you find yourself saying things like these, you finally realize that you have been accepted into your business niche and that your opinions are valid. That is big.

The feeling of belonging is awesome! But please be careful: the acknowledgment that comes from belonging can overinflate your ego and cause you to act up. And that does not apply to artists alone. Anyone who is constantly under media scrutiny because of work – an actress, for instance – will be exposed when she acts out. That could happen to anyone.

To avoid falling into the trap that vanity will insist on setting for you, led by your inner villain, you must focus even closer on your professionalism and latch onto the protagonist inside you with all your might. At times like this, you will be tempted to make crazy demands, convincing yourself that it is absolutely normal. Please, don't go there. Hold on to your therapy sessions and keep your dignity. The villain believes that belonging means being applauded. The protagonist, in turn, knows that belonging means that your talent is being honored. The difference is clear.

Dear reader, I'm sorry, but once you decide to be UNLEASHED, there is no easy way to go about it. Countless women will be looking up to you, so don't screw it up, ok? Of course, you have every right to ask yourself: why would I choose such a difficult path if that's the case? Wouldn't it be better to give up while there's still time? And I'll answer you with another question: if you are not UNLEASHED, what are you going to be? Would you rather spend your entire life dragging your feet, complaining about your luck? Because your villain will, indeed, make you lose so much that you will end up owning regret and disappointment.

To be UNLEASHED, you will also have to build a strong inner foundation so that you're able to get a handle on your emotions whenever you need to. Having it means knowing your vulnerabilities as well as your strengths.

When I speak of big trials, I mean moments when everything is going great at work: your brand is doing well, you are beginning to sell to other countries and position yourself as a market leader, and you start to break the glass ceiling. However, a personal problem arises that will also determine your next steps: a family member gets very sick, an important person in your life dies, your marriage ends, or some other serious event happens that shifts your focus. That's when you may not be able to handle the pressure and ultimately compromise all those years you dedicated to building your business.

You can be sure that those trials will come. I am anticipating them now, not because I am a witch, but because, since I started writing the "Dona de Si" (Unleashed) column for a Brazilian magazine, I have been scanning how things evolve for people who choose to become the protagonists of their own lives, and gathering all that information.

THE BIG CHALLENGE OF LEADERSHIP

I experienced many challenges during my work as the main writer for a major television station in Brazil. The creative work started in 2015 and aired from mid-2016 through early 2017. It was during that production that, after a few years of writing soap operas as a collaborator, co-writer, and performing as an actress, I finally debuted as the head writer, working with a famous TV soap opera writer and a co-writer who was promoted with me (I'll call them Walther and Julio). Of course, I did not reach that place by chance. I have been building my career as a writer since 2004, in the theater, and since 2006, on television. I had been the only actress who was also a soap opera writer for TV Globo. I was very proud of that because I used every opportunity with extreme professionalism in addition to opening the doors to other female colleagues fitting the same profile.

For me, signing a Brazilian soap opera at Globo was the most awesome achievement for the path I had been building. Of course, I had been working with both writers for years by then, and we would try out our triple-leadership on a product we wrote in 2014, which did not make it to production, but during the course of its development, did confirm that there was a good rapport between us.

Triple leadership. Complicated, huh? Until the moment of the BIG TRIAL. Not at all. Our places in the production chain had been well established: W. was the main link, who made the final decisions about everything, J., the backup link, who had a talent for deep perceptions in the drama medium; and me, the production link, had the ability to set up the chapters quickly and to interface with the production and the direction of the soap opera.

It was until we started writing chapter 24 that Julio and I were startled by the news that Walther had been admitted to the intensive care unit of Albert Einstein Hospital in São Paulo. To clarify, the soap opera was not even on the air yet. We were in the process of taping the first chapters when we got this disturbing news.

Julio and I held on tight and kept a steady hand on the steering wheel of that "massive boat" and continued to write the following 18 chapters (from a total of 42 that we had to deliver by the time the soap aired). We would go to the hospital and hold meetings in the intensive care unit. We were determined to preserve the trio's rapport and keep our main link in the production chain. For a few days, we told no one what had happened in the hopes that W. might have a speedy recovery, which had happened on other occasions.

He did recover, in part: he left the hospital in time for the soap opera to be released to the press and worked for a few more days until he was readmitted to the hospital. J. and I continued to believe that we could keep up the original plan, working with our leader from the hospital, until the doctors asked us not to do that anymore. Right then, we realized, as did the tv station, that W. needed to focus on his recovery and not on the soap opera at that moment.

That week, W. returned to the hospital on Tuesday; on Friday, my father was diagnosed with lung cancer that had metastasized to his adrenal gland, combined with pulmonary emphysema; the following Monday, the station decided that I would take over the whole production.

There was my big LEADERSHIP trial. My father was – and still is – a strong presence in my life and everything I had built. And this man, my personal stronghold, was given just one more year to live, at the most. Besides that, the leading writer had been, up until then, my professional guru, the guy who taught me how to develop a soap opera, draft a storyline, negotiate with the production, and coordinate with the direction. Two male figures showed me the ways of life, people with whom I felt safe to grow. Suddenly, both lacked their past strength and had their lives in danger.

After that week of "strong men falling," the soap opera was put entirely under my responsibility. Chapter 20 had already aired, and the ratings were terrible! I believe the storylines portrayed in the soap opera mirrored the real-life chaos experienced by its writers. With the help of the station's artistic direction, we started working in a sort of "production line," where I would draft the storyboard for each chapter, the collaborators would develop the scenes, and my partner would close the chapter. Since we received a public survey, we knew what changes had to be made to draw the audience back – and that's what we did.

Now, you might ask me: "Suzi, how did you not lose it at that time?" My answer is that the one thing that prevented me from giving up was the fact that I had, once again, to draw a line separating my professional from my personal life. At that time, I needed to care for my father and for myself, showing unquestionable professional excellence.

Once I distinguished the significance that my biggest professional challenge had in my life and the weight of my love for my father, I found the strength to carry on, letting nothing fall apart. With that decision, I quelled the panic brought on by picturing life without my father, directed my focus to the story changes needed by the soap opera, and reinforced my leadership skills.

Even though the team had their reservations and apprehensions about such a young female writer. I sharpened the saw of professionalism, and that inner strength alone equipped me to write more than one hundred chapters, deal with yet another illness within the team – Laura Cardoso – and change the descending curve of the ratings, finishing the soap opera at ten points higher than when we took it over.

There, I learned about LEADERSHIP the most: YOU STOP WANTING TO BE; YOU ARE.

That was when my truth set the next steps: I was already screwed up emotionally, and the soap opera was a massive failure. Therefore, I decided to admit it. I tasted the bitter pungency of it and realized the only thing left to do was put my whole heart at the service of the story, and so I did. Once I accepted the truth of the facts, my sense of safety, focus, and work quality surfaced effortlessly.

All I did was allow everything to follow its natural course. I stopped fighting the facts and worked with the serenity that only failure provides. No tantrums, no vanity, no overinflated egos, or moral harassment could disturb me. And so, failure turned into success, just as naturally. Accepting my failures gave me freedom to achieve success.

At times like those, an UNLEASHED woman has to get a grip on her emotions. Remember back in Step 1, when I talked about this? Now, do you see why you need to flex your emotional muscles? So that when you become the main link in your production chain, the team leader, you don't have such a hard time isolating personal feelings and manage to stay focused on belonging. Only then will you have the stamina, the backbone, and the maturity to cross through a deep, rushing, erratic river.

Remember that during the BIG CHALLENGES of our life, those emotional muscles will have to work day and night, and when it's all over, you will have to take excellent care of them. That is because the emotional upheaval will take its toll when the storm passes. And, dear reader, this is a fight for the fearless, the committed, and the resilient.

At the end of that writing journey, I blacked out on the day I delivered the final chapter. I passed out like a "Battlefield

Cinderella," and then, without waiting to be kissed by a prince, I awoke and proceeded to take care of my emotional state, which was so tattered. By that time, my father had already beat the oncologist's prognosis and was in excellent health and in great spirits, which allowed me to go away on a trip.

I traveled to a remote beach in the State of Bahia (which is the place where I go to reconnect) and slept better than ever, cried more than ever, allowed myself to feel new, beautiful feelings, and returned with a burning question: Who had I become after all that? When I soul-searched about "all that," I was not referring just to my work on the soap opera, but to my whole journey, from when I was 15 until that moment. I recalled the major events, achievements, and defeats and pondered about who I was in the midst of so many characters that I had performed and also created. Who was I in this life that I dedicated so much to building my own path? Who had I become?

My desire to write remained, but it was no longer fiction. I wanted to write about my experiences as a woman up until that point. I had reached a professional place where I would look around me and see no other women. Were we not allowed to be like Tina Fey or Michaela Coel in Brazil? Actresses who produced their own content? Perhaps.

I was not satisfied with how I perceived women in the job market. Many actresses wrote, just like I did. Why weren't they there with me, writing storylines, too? Why didn't we see women in certain jobs? Why weren't there black female leaders in a number of professions? The questioner in me had been activated, and I only wanted to reflect on this with potential readers.

This desire drove me to ask my press assistant at the time to schedule a conversation between Marina Caruso, then the director of Marie Claire magazine, and me, so I could tell her that I wanted to write about female professional growth. Marina jumped at the idea, offered me a column, and even asked if I had a title in mind. I promptly replied: "Dona de Si" (Unleashed). The next week, I debuted the column, and in just a few months, it was a hit. Later came the talks, the licensing of the brand, and, finally, the institute (@institutodonadesi).

This was yet another turning point in my life. A turning point that only happens to people who face their BIG CHALLENGE and realize that LEADERSHIP has nothing to do with the group you belong to, but rather with yourself, with the pursuit of your journey, the place that produces the fuel that will drive you: your truth.

STEP 4 – WHAT HAVE I LEARNED AFTER SO MANY STRUGGLES?

In 2017, I started writing the "Dona de Si" (Unleashed) column for Marie Claire magazine. In 2019, I moved it to Vogue, and in 2021 to Forbes. What motivated me to write for the female audience was the desire to understand the women I wanted to speak to. The decision to change outlets was made specifically to reach out to women in different segments with diverse beliefs and to speak to all of them. I created an e-mail for our communications and replied to all the messages that came in. That exchange made me a better writer, helped me understand the common female problems within the job market, and I was able to pinpoint our shared hardships.

After six months and more than twenty pieces, I understood what I had built up to that point: my unique, unprecedented path, which I found to be invaluable, built with just a handful of concessions (I will elaborate on this later on). Finally, I looked back and saw the magnitude of what I had done with myself: from the little girl who danced on the balcony to the "DONA DE SI" (Unleashed) book and foundation. That was a fact. I had not only managed to pay my bills but also dared to develop a professional signature, giving authorship to my work. That excellence makes me immensely proud.

Everything that I decided to do, or was hired to do, came out better than I expected, and that was always a personal, strategic choice I made. It also included saying "no" to jobs that would not afford me the space to outdo myself – making that absolutely clear to the person who asked me.

In everything to which I said yes, I plunged, challenged myself, learned, grew, got crushed, knocked down, and got back on my feet. I qualify this process as daring because I had managed to prove that, even though I had a nice Latina body, I also had a brain. Although I am an actress, I am an excellent writer. In addition to being an artist, I also am a full-fledged entrepreneur. I did not break after three years, which is why, on countless occasions, I was the only woman in the places where I would find myself.

Women in Spaces of Power

I must admit that being the sole woman in those spaces of power filled me with immense pride, to the point that I teetered on the edge of the QUEEN BEE SYNDROME (this has nothing to do with Beyonce, ok). This syndrome refers to a situation where a woman reaches a leadership position and strives to maintain her exclusivity as the only female in order to uphold her status. But I did not allow myself to fall into that trap and understood that the column had to serve women's interests, to show all women that they could climb the broken steps of our professional advancement and shatter the glass ceiling.

Dearest reader, please understand that feeling disappointed with the "boys' club" that exists everywhere and watching contracts awarded to less qualified men will deplete your energy. That being said, it is time to understand how to avoid all this backward behavior.

The weekly exercise of writing the column helped me to see where, during my journey, I had walked on the broken step and, at times, been forced to hang on to the handrail with just one hand. I was kicked out of the game on many occasions, but I always found my way back in. It's exhausting. At one point, I got fed up with all the rubbish, so the "Dona de Si" (Unleashed) column became my getaway, where I could write freely about it as honestly as I could. I am sure that attitude attracted so many readers to the column.

In 2017, when my column debuted, there wasn't much space in the press dedicated to the female audience addressing entrepreneurship; the few that existed were not published in women's fashion magazines but in in The Economist, Forbes, and Time. I wanted to reach an audience that craved material on the subject, women who were anxious to share their stories with me and shout: "I experience that every single day!"

This combination of joy and pain made "DONA DE SI" (UNLEASHED) successful, not to mention that it was the first enterprise I did not plan. After all, I just wanted to write a column. Within five years, it had grown into a brand with products (registered with the Brazilian Patent and Trademark Office – INPI, in several categories), a talk, a workshop, a business course, merchandise, a concept (selling a real woman), a gender diversity consulting business, an Institute, and this book.

The business overran me: either I kept up with its growth, or that speeding train would run me over. And, of course, not only did I keep up with all of that, I got the UNLEASHED train up to a good speed. I knew that the column was a success when UNLEASHED earned a blurb on the cover of Globo newspaper's online version every week. It was the first time my writing received more attention than pictures of me in a bikini on a beach. That was an accomplishment I have always pursued. No, I have never wanted to make my body invisible, but I have always wanted to give that body a VOICE, and that was finally happening. I was creating a female awareness movement, which showed the power of our VOICE.

Vogue Brazil

A VOICE is something we carry inside us, like a core belief, and in order to communicate, we require a big dose of self-esteem and self-reliance while dealing with fear and risk assessment. No problem! I was ready to show more of myself. And the time came when my voice needed more nourishment to make a difference.

Through the "Dona De Si" column, a heartfelt conversation unfolded with my readers, revealing a new path, something bigger than just purpose. It became a mission. Yes, a mission to empower whoever I could, not with orders or catchy phrases, but with genuine humanity; recognizing that success is defined on their own terms. It's about their personal growth and triumphs. From that point on, I no longer felt like a solitary woman because I had readers to fight for. I had a reason to grace the red carpet, and it wasn't just about appearance but about delivering a powerful message. Ever since, life has guided me to transform the message of UNLEASHED women into meaningful ACTION, liberating as many allies as possible.

STEP 5 – WHAT AM I GOING TO LEAVE TO THE WORLD?

When I reached this step, my issue was no longer about investing in myself or discovering what I could achieve professionally. At this point, I was famous in Brazil, could buy all the clothes I wanted, and had a collection of very expensive handbags and a stable professional career. My issue now was: what am I going to leave to the world? That is called a legacy, something you do for the collective good, which can impact several generations. Goodness! All those years ago, all I wanted to do was dance on balconies, and now here I was, pondering about legacy.

Now, that's a journey, a path built and still under construction because my carving for renewal is what keeps me going. I began asking myself: "What can I do for people? How can I help make the world a better place?"

My aspiration was pretty obvious to me: to help promote gender equality in the job market. But I knew that simply writing the column or selling a product would not have the impact that my heart desired. That's when, after much rumination, I woke up one night around three a.m. with the whole idea for the "Dona de Si" Institute in my head. I finally realized what my legacy to the world should be: to advance the careers of extremely talented women who were constantly crashing into the glass ceiling.

The "Dona de Si" Institute was not born out of a desire to do charity but rather out of the determination to prepare leaders, to make women the protagonists of their own lives. I wanted to work with groups of women who usually go unnoticed, stuck in the same place their entire lives instead of moving forward. I saw it happen in the entertainment industry (where the institute had its kick start), and I realized that the problem was never competence, but self-esteem, self-reliance, dominion over one's territory, and the struggle for protagonism.

I was enraged with the "white boys' club" in the Brazilian entertainment industry because I had just been a victim of that system. I did everything I could to associate myself with the women behind the work: those who created but did not sign their creations; those who wrote an entire paper but didn't get credit for it; those who managed but remained assistants. Because there was always a man granting them the space, they should feel obligated to thank him for the opportunity to be there. Oh, come on, you jerks!

The first thing I did was to write an entire column on the issue of misogyny within the Brazilian entertainment industry, without naming names but delivering a strong message that soon spread throughout the market. It became clear in that article that I would no longer accept the place they wanted to force me to stay in. By making that clear, I hoped to encourage other professionals to do the same. Thereby inching towards the end of the abuses perpetrated: both moral and sexual. To begin to act – because action is all I believe in – I decided not to touch my savings but find some way to be the first to invest in my dream, and – voilà! – the idea came to me. Why not sell those luxury handbags that were just sitting in my closet and were expensive as hell?

THE STORY BEHIND THE SALE OF THE CHANEL HANDBAGS

I owned a collection of Chanel handbags, which I assembled over time to validate my success. After taking care of more significant expenses, I would treat myself to a new one with every major job I landed. That was my reward system for a few years, but it no longer made sense even though I loved them. I don't know; they seemed obsolete, ready to be recycled and turned into something bigger. So, it was done.

There was an additional detail that hastened the sale of those expensive handbags: the creative director of the brand in question, Mr. Karl Lagerfeld, was alive and made some blunt statements about the #metoo movement, going as far as saying that we, women, were used to being harassed and that the hashtag would amount to nothing, except for the termination of the careers of some brilliant photographers. I could understand the fact that an elderly man had that kind of opinion, but I did not understand – and I still don't – the fact that the brand didn't refute his statements. That broke my heart.

When I saw this discrepancy between what the brand stood for and its attitude toward that statement, I chose to have my institute and promised never again to buy anything sold by brands with misogynist, homophobic or racist inclinations. That is what I have been trying to do. That is conscientious consumerism, motivated by the conviction that it is our buying power that allows anything to exist. Please, remember that.

Back to the story: I took those twelve handbags, advertised them on BagMe, a luxury e-commerce channel, sold all of them, and invested the money in the institute throughout its first year of operation. That is how everything started. I hired a lawyer and an accountant to set things up lawfully, just as I had done with my production company in the past. Actually, even better, because this time I had experience. In addition to having all of the institute's paperwork up and running, I had also registered the "Dona de Si" trademark with the Brazilian Intellectual Property Institute – INPI. Dearest reader, it is crucial that you register your trademark and never copy the name of an existing one.

I started off by helping to advance women whose talent I already knew and who were suffering from the limitations imposed upon them by the industry: Clara Sória, Tatiana Tibúrcio, and Luana Xavier. The first two are screenwriters and directors; the third one is an actress and TV host. After five years since we first began, the three of them are enjoying tremendous success.

The advancements consisted of supporting Tatiana in the production of the series pilot that she had developed, *A face negra do amor* (The dark side of love); investing in the documentary produced by Clara Sória about Leona Vingativa; and following Luana's career helping her leverage her visibility and supporting her in the productions in which she was involved.

Additionally, in association with Amir Slama, we released a line of bodysuits for all sizes. At our show at São Paulo Fashion Week, we introduced real diversity and inclusion on the runway for the first time: with real women of all sizes – from 36 to 56 – lovely, fulfilled, and UNLEASHED. It was a huge success, putting the institute on the radar of possible sponsoring brands – crucial to our projects.

"DONA DE SI" (UNLEASHED) IS IN FASHION

From that point on, I understood that we were ready to grow and move on to the next step: expanding the team. I hired two professionals: a manager and a specialist in social responsibility, who collaborated with the design and the budgeting of all of my dreams. Then, we got into public notices and incentive laws, and I threw myself into meetings with brands to introduce the institute. Things heated up after I talked with my dear friend Maythê Birman about the "DONA DE SI" (Unleashed) project, and she introduced me to the Arezzo CEO: Ale Birman, who loved the idea of preparing female leaders. The institute's first initiative was implemented through Arezzo&Co, which changed the lives of many women with that effort.

We created the Screenwriting Contest with a clear purpose: to change the lives of all the women who entered! Selling shoes would be a consequence of an empathetic, transformative action. That is the publicity I believe in.

It was a project that we are extremely proud of: 1st Film Contest for Women - Arezzo Dona de Si. It was a five-minute screenplay writing contest open to women all around the country. Five winners, one from each region of Brazil, would have their films produced as the "High Summer Season 2020" Campaign for Arezzo, referencing the theme of female protagonism. More than three hundred screenplays were entered, and the winners (Mirtes Santana, Claudia Roberta, Ana Celia Costa, Samira Ramalho, and Angélica Rodrigues) came to Rio de Janeiro to experience the "DONA DE SI" (Unleashed) TRANSFORMATIVE JOURNEY in addition to a mentoring program to help with their scripts. After that, we taped the five films under my artistic direction.

THE UNLEASHED SCREENWRITERS FROM THE AREZZO CAMPAIGN

Our team and cast focused on inclusion, with a nearly equal number of white and black women in positions of leadership on set and acting. Established actresses, who are seldom asked to do campaigns, participated in the pictures and films. The absolute protagonists were: Luana Xavier, Letícia Karneiro, Tatá Lopes, Julie Nakayama, and the biggest star: missus Léa Garcia.

UNLEASHED + AREZZO

We held openings in two movie theaters: one in Rio de Janeiro and another in São Paulo. Later, the campaign went to the brand's stores throughout Brazil, boosting the visibility of the institute's work and the screenwriters and actresses. Arezzo also benefitted from a 90% increase in traffic on its marketplace, reaching over 40 million impacts with the digital campaign on social media. It was a home run for the consolidation of #ArezzoJuntas because the project was, in fact, executed with women united so that everything would work out, and that ultimately happened. A few months after that project, I was invited by Africa agency to speak on Africa Talks about the "Dona de Si" + Arezzo case. I heard the word CASE OF SUCESS from the biggest advertising agency in Brazil. That changed everything for me.

On Africa Talks, I spoke on behalf of IDS, and Raissa, marketing manager, spoke on behalf of Arezzo; we explained the whole development of the campaign, how it was done, and the results produced to an audience of account managers and creative service agents, who wanted to understand how we had managed to combine brand purpose and product so smoothly, in a single action. The path of the "Dona de Si" Institute had become clear: we found out how to execute major projects and cause huge impacts on the audience, and we would go on from there.

After Arezzo, we worked with Brazil Foundation, which was interested in infusing diversity and a more modern feel into its annual celebration. I set up a team of screenwriters "advanced" by the institute, and we created an incredibly beautiful and astounding video showing a SORORITY CIRCLE formed by the awarded women. Additionally, we wrote the entire award speech, ditching all the stiffness and highlighting the assertiveness of the actions for the benefit of women.

GETTING BACK TO THE INSTITUTE'S DAY-TO-DAY IMPACT

As I mentioned in Step 4, the five screenwriters who won the Arezzo Contest saw a significant change in their lives after the "DONA DE SI" (Unleashed) TRANSFORMATIVE JOURNEY, the contents of which I will proceed to describe. It is a training in entrepreneurship that teaches ALL WOMEN to get out of their VILLAIN mode and come into contact with the PROTAGONIST inside, with theoretical and practical classes created by Virginia de Gomez and myself. You can follow the American launch of the UNLEASHED TRANSFORMATIVE JOURNEY in English by accessing our Instagram @unleashedfoundation.

Any woman who decides to experience the training at the institute will have access to the following modules, which spell out the original Portuguese name "DONA DE SI."

1. D: development on a personal level
2. O: organization and planning
3. N: natural approach to your own talent
4. A: asserting your power
5. D: discovery and analysis of the industry
6. E: empathy
7. S: segmentation
8. I: intelligence to deal with emotions (emotional intelligence).

Each module is split into chapters:
1. DEVELOPMENT ON A PERSONAL LEVEL:
    1. Health;
    2. Financial security;
    3. Healthy relationships;
    4. Authenticity in her beauty;
    5. General knowledge.

2. ORGANIZATION AND PLANNING:
    1. Financial plan;
    2. Time organization and management.

3. NATURAL APPROACH TO YOUR OWN TALENT:
    1. Digital marketing;
    2. Self-recording class;
    3. How to develop a social project.

4. ASSERTING YOUR POWER:
    1. Leadership.

5. DISCOVERY AND ANALYSIS OF THE MARKET:
   1. Learning market research;
   2. How to come out ahead of the competition.

6. EMPATHY:
   1. Sorority in practice.

7. SEGMENTATION:
   1. How to map out your public.

8. INTELLIGENCE TO DEAL WITH EMOTIONS (EMOTIONAL INTELLIGENCE):
   1. Positive psychology.

The entire training program was based on the Maslow pyramid and included a distance learning methodology for adult women, including assignments, actions, and goals to be monitored. The life change is instantaneous.

MASLOW PYRAMID

Created by psychologist Abraham H. Maslow, the pyramid is a schematic illustrating a hierarchic division where the needs perceived as lower level must be met before those perceived as higher. Maslow defined a series of five types of human needs, arranged as follows:

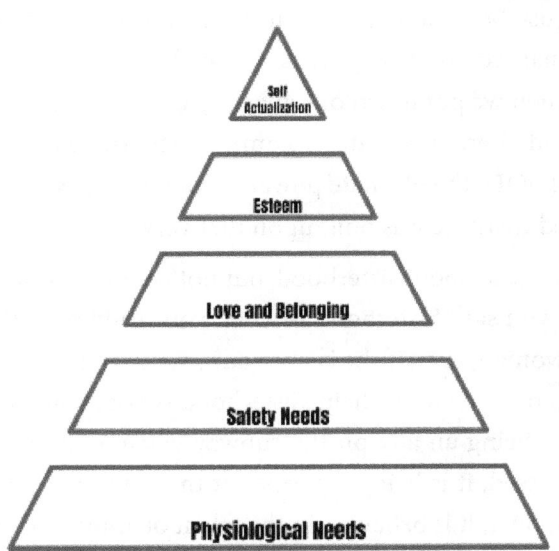

The UNLEASHED TRANSFORMATIVE JOURNEY makes you the master of your destiny and empowers you to choose your way with a financial and business plan conceived for the female reality. We prepare women to be the leaders of their own lives, happier, with more money in the bank, and filled with purpose. Moreover, every woman embarking on the Unleashed Journey receives dedicated support from social workers and therapists, ensuring they feel heard and empowered.

SISTERHOOD

The perspective filled with love and trust in the full female potential only came to me when I started to practice and believe in the alliance among women. We were made to be sisters and partners, not to fear one another. We must stop judging another woman just because she is wearing an outfit we don't like, or lipstick that we don't find attractive, or because she has a weird laugh. When we put down our guard against another woman and understand her, we can become partners. That is called SISTERHOOD, the ultimate power a woman can experience. The Unleashed Institute was built upon that very foundation.

Much is said about sisterhood, but not enough is done about it, wouldn't you say? Sisterhood is when you really pay attention to another woman, even if she is not your friend, and truly care if she is all right or if she needs help. Sisterhood is not about being BFFs, it is about being an ally on the subway when another woman is being harassed, it is being a partner at the conference table when men encircle it, it is believing in the talent of another woman, and above all, it is turning all of that into ACTION. That is what the Unleashed Institute advances: connections among women to be a space of creation where everyone can fully express their potential and, in doing so, collaborate with each other. When one of us faces a challenge, we exchange ideas, the issues are more easily resolved, and building a path grows more pleasurable.

The "Dona de Si" (Unleashed) Institute in Brazil was doing really well, with countless actions and sponsorships all set to go until…

THE PANDEMIC HIT, BRINGING CHALLENGES TO OVERCOME AND SO MANY QUESTIONS TO ANSWER

How would we keep the "Dona de Si" Institute? How would we reach those who had not yet become UNLEASHED? How would we support one another so that none of us disappeared? How would each of us keep their light shining? How would we handle our team in this new scenario?

We would probably have closed if we did not find quick answers to these questions, but no one on the institute's team allowed that to happen. I managed to negotiate everyone's salaries because working for free is not allowed here, we lowered the monthly fee and had the idea to create a SELF-SUSTAINABLE INSTITUTE. How? By taking it into the digital universe.

But first, it is important that you know: the day after the complete lockdown, we were contacted by women desperate for mentoring programs and offered several free of charge, which saved many businesses from bankruptcy. Additionally, we did live broadcasts of classes on how to proceed in negotiations, enter into partnerships, and manage the biggest crisis of the 21st century so far.

What was the result of all that? Here are some cases of micro-entrepreneurs whose businesses we helped save with our free mentoring programs during the worst moment of the coronavirus pandemic.

ANYONE WHO IS UNLEASHED IS A LEADER, SO…

…it was my responsibility to encourage my team and make a plan so that we could continue to exist. That was when sisterhood spoke volumes: everyone came together, made concessions, and we managed to get the institute's PLATFORM online, including on it the whole "DONA DE SI" TRANSFORMATIVE JOURNEY for a very low price so that any woman could have access to the classes and the entrepreneur training.

For the women who could not afford to pay 50 *reais* (10 dollars) a month for the training, we created the "Dona de Si Ambassador Program," where a successful woman covered the cost for five, ten, twenty, or even fifty women to access the platform. We had a database with the names of informal micro-entrepreneurs who needed this help and included them, little by little, in the groups supported by each ambassador.

I started spreading the word about this program through my WhatsApp account. In two months, we had secured free access to the platform for two hundred women, with the help of ambassadors Antônia Frering, Mariliz Pereira Jorge, Maria Elizabete Carvalho, Sigrid Dias, Angélica, Flavio Garcia da Rocha, Ana Paula Araújo, Kênia Maria, Ana Zamper, Cleo, Lu Rodrigues, Silvia Machado, Flavia Camanho, Lais Trajano, in addition to the first brand that joined us in this effort: *Cidade Jardim* Shopping Mall, which supported twenty women from the fashion industry.

Outside of the Ambassador Program, we sold an average of two subscriptions per day for the journey. Today there are more than five hundred women studying on our platform, where they have access to private live broadcasts with me so they can ask me questions, besides the groups set up on WhatsApp where we celebrate victories and help one other. Six months after a tough battle to keep my dream alive, we were finally alive again!

I wrote "my dream," but I should correct that: today, the "Dona de Si" Institute is my whole team's dream. Our 14 amazing women are groundbreaking professionals in their fields, and nearly all of them left major corporations in search of an occupation that would allow them to make good money, especially bringing a lot of purpose to their day-to-day lives. We have former *Embratel*,

Rede Globo, and *Vale* employees, as well as women who experienced the journey and then came to work with us. There are no words to express my joy.

The pandemic tested the resilience of all teams, especially leaders. I realized that, in the new economic scenario, the task of leading must be shared with all the people who work with you, no matter if they are two, three, thirty, or one hundred. You will remain the protagonist (and liable for the price payable for it), but you must give your team space to express how they were impacted by the crisis because only then will they be able to support one other mutually.

As of 2022, seeing people exclusively from a professional viewpoint will no longer be possible. We must also consider their peculiarities and subjectivities. Information such as where they live and who they live with, if they have children or elderly parents, among other aspects of people's personal lives, will be relevant because sisterhood exists in the smallest details. That will be crucial for any UNLEASHED who wants to survive in the post-pandemic era.

On your team, there will be real people rather than mere workers; people fight with their partners, they lose loved ones, they sometimes get into abusive relationships, their heads go to bad places, then they get better, but the fact is that you will never again be able to pretend that you don't see the effect that all of this can have on a professional level. It is important to have this information to assess how the pandemic has affected each person who works with you and needs help, which could be a health treatment, if your company can afford it, or a few days off to reset, for instance.

Here, the difference between an UNLEASHED entrepreneur and an entrepreneur without her training becomes apparent. The man comes in and says, without flinching: "We have to cut costs." For women, it is very hard to do that. We want to manage everything, even if we end up blowing it. A major reason why many women face failure around the third anniversary of their business is our unwavering determination to hold the fort for everyone.

I will say this again: you are not everyone's mother. You are the owner of your business. You are the entrepreneur of your own life. And, to implement that, you do not have to distance yourself from people. Numbers have nothing to do with being cold. Numbers are people, and numbers are your team. So, if you have a secretary that makes X, you will have to find a way to cut her salary by half so that you do not have to terminate her employment. By acting this way, you keep your inner light on. This was how I managed to keep working until the economy got back on track. I tried to preserve my team and my business. The solution I found to avoid bankruptcy was not firing people but renegotiating expectations with my teams and brand partners.

I own a company. I have been the entrepreneur of my life since the age of 15. I have always managed my teams. Today, I have partners and collaborators, I am at a different moment in my corporate career, and I can say a few things for sure:

POINT 1: the world's money is not going to run out

It has never run out; not even during the Great Depression of 1929, which is considered the worst, longest period of economic recession of the capitalist system of the 20th Century. What does happen is that money changes hands. Every hundred years or so, some event in human history causes money to flow differently.

During the French Revolution, when the nobility's heads were cut off, the money went to the hands of the working class, who would become the owners of banks and large companies, which, in turn, went broke during the crisis of 1929. Later came the Second World War, which produced yet another terrible crisis. And so, from one crisis to another, we arrive in 2008, when Lehman Brothers, one of the most traditional investment banks of the United States, went bankrupt, causing the stock market to plummet around the world and other banks to lose billions of dollars. Then, in 2020, came the coronavirus pandemic.

After these crises that we experienced, money changed hands again. It will shift from the hands of those unwilling to change their way of relating to clients and employees. In the world of today, the patriarchal economy is losing ground. Nowadays, no one joins a company planning to stay there for fifty years. Every person has to be the owner of their own professional path and, for tax purposes, have a corporate identity, just as they have a personal identity. That is why the Individual Micro-Entrepreneur Program (MEI) in Brazil is so important: it legitimizes an individual's personal identity as a corporate identity, for tax purposes, without binding the individual to incorporate a legal entity. The *MEI* allows you to work.

When money changes hands, the way that people relate to each other changes as well. During the age of Monarchy, there was no such thing as climbing the social ladder. You were either an aristocrat or a commoner. There was a huge gap between those two classes, and the working class ultimately occupied that space between nobility and bastards. Today, the world's biggest problem is the massive disparity between the middle and poor classes. It is precisely in that gap that money will accumulate since consumption has not stopped, and it will not stop. And that is going to happen through a new connection to be forged among people.

POINT 2: our worst enemy is despair

At some point, everyone has been in a bad place, even those born extremely wealthy. I myself have lived with zero stability, depending on my play's ticket sales to pay the bills. The fact is that no one in the world is assured a smooth ride.

Dear reader, when despair hits, cry it out, get all your emotions out, but do not believe that the game is over for you, and do not leave the playing field. The ball is still rolling. The thing that is going to keep you on your feet is your new project. If you bet on it, you will keep your fire burning, your emotional fabric will mature, and you will be able to understand the new economic framework that is coming.

Our female emotional side must be used in our favor. Our emotions run high, we cry, and we are highly intuitive. It is no longer appropriate to believe that your sensitivity is causing you to see something that no one else sees and that, as a result, you might be called crazy. Now is the time for women to break down the doors. The patriarchal economy is going to lose money. A man who believes that thousands of deaths caused by a virus do not matter is not going to survive in the new economic order. We are not numbers. We are hearts that beat. The time has come to find new references.

POINT 3: what is the new strategy?

The comfort zone has been obliterated. Even if the coronavirus had not appeared, some other change could have happened and affected everyone. A change had already been knocking on our doors for a while. The strategy to survive in the new world is loyalty. You might think that is silly when we speak of money, but I can assure you it is not. What matters now is that you know your client's pain (or your employer's pain) and your own pain so that you can help each other. The coronavirus has affected us all, but the aches differ. Ask yourself: what is your ache now? What challenges are you facing at the moment?

Only those who understand that sometimes losing money means earning the client's loyalty, regardless of the size of the business, will stay on their feet. In the new economic scenario, there is no space left for exploiters. We are all on the same boat and must be flexible when negotiating. We must learn emotional self-management.

In the world's new economic order, we all cry and dry each other's tears, creating a chain of loyalty among people to rebuild the economy. Instead of financial gain, the primary value is the service and behavior toward the client and anyone, including ourselves. It is there that we should place our hopes. Sure, this change is still happening, and the road might be a long one. The same goes for women's rights.

HOW CAN WE HACK THE SYSTEM?

The job market is simply an extension of an old-time fair in the middle of the town square, where one person sells and another buys, thus making the economy tick. The problem is that the rules governing that market were made by the people who created it: white, heterosexual males. Women, black and Lgbtqa+ people, were left out of the economy: white women were meant to be procreating wives; black women, to be workers; black males, to carry heavy loads; and, among the homosexuals, women became prostitutes used for orgies, and men were just degenerates who were better off dead.

South America was also built on the foundations of this colonial system, and that was how we separated the more noble areas from the poor areas, split the countries between the poor (blacks) and the rich (whites), and stripped women of any and all public power. And what happens now? Those who were never accepted into the "market" insisted, hacked the system, and managed to get in and excel after a long, hard fight. However, not many were that lucky, and that triggered another problem: the impression that the women and/or the black people who reached high-ranking positions did so because they are extraordinarily talented. No! Those people had to make concessions. They had to emulate masculine behaviors or whiten their résumés in order to fit into the "club."

With the pandemic, that lie-ridden boiling pot exploded. It was the spark that had been missing to make women understand the lie they had been living, believing they were given the same opportunities as men; but it was mostly the racial boiling pot that exploded right in our middle-class faces. George Floyd lit a small fire with his tragic, unfair murder. Today, we are experiencing the opening of the "business market" to effectively include the black community through companies like Magalu, which announced that it would only hire black employees to work as trainees in 2021 in an initiative called "affirmative action." An action conceived to counteract the accumulated effects of past discrimination. High praise to Magalu for understanding the importance of transforming its own "job market" into a space that fits everyone.

The system, the rules, procedures, and protocols are made up and organized by the owners of the money, who, despite all the movements for inclusion, are still white males. So, in order for you, dear reader, to exist on the market and attract investments in your business, you have to learn how to hack into this system, which is still the prevailing system, even though it is in transformation.

If we abstain from penetrating the system, we will lose everything we have achieved so far. The awareness that the money that comes into your hands belongs to someone else, in this case, a white male, is crucial for understanding the difficulties you will face. And, especially, how you will overcome them. The concentration of the world's wealth in the hands of 2% of people with common gender and racial traits is the big abusive relationship we face daily. It is not just you. It is all of us. And, together, we are stronger.

This is SISTERHOOD.

MULTIPLYING

HOW I PENETRATED THE SYSTEM AND CHANGED IT

As mentioned, the play Up Close She Ain't Normal! took off my acting and writing career. In 2015, I sold the idea to produce a film based on the play to TV Globo and got the green light to start working on the screenplay. I wrote the rough draft – for those of you not familiar with the field, this means the first iteration of what will become a final draft of the screenplay. Very well, with that material in hand, I went after a script doctor, which is someone who improves an existing screenplay. Unfortunately, that didn't happen. Quite the contrary. I was informed that the film would no longer be produced.

Because I believe that the word *no* only exists if I allow it to, I followed my instincts and enrolled in a course on screenwriting for film taught by an American, where I was able to apply everything I learned during the second draft of my project, which improved considerably from the first one. I submitted the screenplay for consideration, and again I received "No" as an answer. No from them because I continued to say "Yes" to myself.

One day, life put me in contact with a successful film producer at the time, who agreed to read my script, and just one day later, he called me back to say that he wanted to produce it. YES! The *no* was beginning to turn into a *yes*. However, one of the cogs in the film's machinery did not believe I could author a screenplay and demanded that another scriptwriter be hired. Since I was extremely busy writing a soap opera, I agreed and handed the material to that professional.

Six months later, I got back a script that had everything except the story of my play. The protagonist, originally a woman fighting to "make it," had been turned into a floozy interested in nabbing a rich husband, and Aunt Suelly died in the new story. What? That was not my film. After much discussion, they agreed to hire another screenwriter to collaborate with me in writing the script, and that solution turned out even worse. The guy would freak out every time I touched the screenplay, and he turned my story, which was recommended for all audiences, into an adult movie, including an orgy. What?

In that production stage, we already had a distributor who owned the film since he put in the most money, so I decided to show the distributor what had been done to the story of the play he had watched and bought. He supported me and agreed that I be put in charge of the screenplay. I managed to write the screenplay that would ultimately be filmed with the help of my team – Martha Mendonça and Renato Santos.

It took three years for someone to believe I could write the screenplay for the story I had created! Now, isn't male chauvinism or misogyny to blame for that?

After much fighting and gaining some enemies along the way, I finally made the film with the cast of my dreams and an amazing crew. I also managed to approve an inclusion rider for the film, which is when the protagonist (also an associate producer of the film) asks the production company that the crew and cast be selected according to the diversity in society. As a result, we managed to cut through some roadblocks. For instance, in the soundtrack, editing, and in the casting of black actors to play rich and powerful characters. We broke the pattern of casting only white males from the neighborhood of Leblon (a rich place in Rio) in those roles in major Brazilian productions. That made me very, very happy.

The result was a mainstream film, but a film with its own unique signature. That is the kind of quality that I am interested in delivering to the audience. It may not be the easiest road, but it is the most beautiful. And the result?

I made a film about that play in which I invested 3 thousand *reais* (1 thousand dollars) all those years ago. Fifteen years later, it became a big film, and I made a point of including women in all of its stages: from the screenwriting to the heads of the directing and producing crews and the soundtrack team. Everything. I wanted to break paradigms within the movie industry, starting with the prejudice they showed against the fact that I was the scriptwriter.

Up Close She Ain't Normal! is a film with a big budget for Brazilian standards. It was one of the biggest releases of 2020, making a lot of money and multiplying my initial investment by more than ten thousand times. That is proof of success, tenacity, and steadfast commitment to my dream and making it come true. But, most of all, it reflects my absolute potential to create a journey capable of transforming the lives of thousands of women. It also reflects the respect I have for my childhood dreams as a young girl and for your dreams as well, dearest reader.

Unleashed

Movie Poster UP CLOSE SHE AIN'T NORMAL

Expanding My Territory

Since 2020, when I parted ways with my Rede Globo as a writer, I poured my heart and soul into translating a project that resonates deeply with me: Woman Inc, a series tackling workplace abusive practices. Little did I know, an English studio had been on the hunt for a project about women from a Latina author, and my name easily caught their attention upon arrival in Brazil.

Following initial meetings, we hammered out the contract terms, and it hit me: I was embarking on a journey to work for a global audience right in the heart of Los Angeles. After navigating through various bureaucratic hoops, here I am now, armed with three additional creation contracts, collaborating with major studios, and preparing to launch this book in English.

What's truly magical is that five years ago, I could never have imagined the extent to which my life would expand at the age of 45. These days, I'm learning invaluable lessons within the confines of American writers' rooms, and my next milestone will be stepping foot onto a film set right here. What drives this expansion is the message I carry, one of the empowered women who are truly aware of their paths and actively working to forge them.

In addition to working with Avalon Studios and Amazon Studios, I also landed a gig at DISNEY PLUS, bringing to life the brand's first Latina villain in the upcoming series A MAGIA DE ARUNA, set to premiere worldwide in 2023. As the clock struck midnight on the cusp of 2022 and 2023, I retreated into solitude, making a personal pact with the forces of life to embrace whatever the Universe had in store for me. I realized there was so much more to explore and experience. And indeed, there is.

Even while based in Los Angeles, I keep all my projects in Brazil alive and kicking. I'm currently wrapping up two scripts targeted at the Latin market. One of them is the highly anticipated sequel to Up Close She Ain't Normal! which is turning into a franchise. The other project involves adapting my partner and incredible writer Thalita Reboucas' book, *Adultos Sem Filtro*.

One of my biggest concerns was ensuring the Unleashed Institute thrived, even beyond the borders of Brazil. So, I went the extra mile to assemble the best team possible, and it paid off. While venturing into new territories to spread the UNLEASHED message, the Institute continues to empower and transform the lives of over five hundred women back home in Brazil annually.

This year, we have three major projects in full swing: Unleashed Transformative Journey Casas Bahia - empowering three hundred women with our entrepreneurship method; Fashion Unleashed Lab Animale - training sixty women in the entrepreneurial journey, along with sewing and fashion design skills to create collections for fashion shows; and Unleashed PRIO - equipping one hundred and twenty women with entrepreneurial skills, digital marketing assistance gel manicure techniques, lymphatic drainage massage therapy, and hair braiding.

In all of these projects, 75% of the women we serve are talented black, from the *Morro dos Prazeres Community*, as well as women from Porto Alegre and Bahia. Despite their talents, they lack the opportunities and pathways for growth. What the institute accomplishes through its initiatives is providing a platform for these women to enter the market with our unwavering support and guidance.

In addition to the entrepreneurial training and hands-on labs, we also offer therapy and psychiatric support through our partner SAS Brasil, to ensure the mental well-being of our students. Given the alarming statistics, my goal for 2024 is to renew sponsorships, secure more funding to empower a greater number of women in Brazil, and hire lawyers to tackle domestic violence cases.

Furthermore, in 2024, our entire platform and training materials will be available in English, allowing women worldwide to access the Unleashed method.

In Brazil, the Unleashed lectures are topping the charts, reaching cities where women have never had exposure to a culture of female empowerment. My mission is to serve as a new guiding light of beliefs and establish thriving communities of women entrepreneurs in those regions. This movement is set to revolutionize the country's economy. That's my estimation.

Unleashed

Life is incredible. My heart is overflowing with joy as I have the opportunity to share this with you and other women who will read this book. This is the story of my journey, which at 46 years old, is just getting started. I've been embracing happiness and fulfillment but also fighting relentlessly. Always striving for our place in the world. My next big milestone is founding the Unleashed Foundation here in the United States to empower young Latina, Black, and transgender women in technical roles within the film industry. It's all about being Unleashed. So, how about you? Are you ready to join me?

LET'S GET PRACTICAL

Now is the time for you to put your steps into action toward a whole new world where you take charge. This section of the book is all about the practical side of being truly Unleashed. Come on! It's going to be incredible. #UNLEASHED

When I first started the Institute, I needed to map out why women are so prone to give up on the construction of our professional life.

I found studies of all kinds: women are more educated, make more profit when leading, and are more enterprising. We are capable and brave. Ok. So, what was the cause of such a devastating outcome and a high number of female entrepreneurs going broke? That answer I could not find anywhere. Therefore, I decided to conduct my own study and relied on my readers.

We identified the three major challenges women encounter in the workplace, and they have nothing to do with their professional skills but rather with cultural factors. The three main causes leading to professional bankruptcy and surrender among women are:

FEMALE OVERBURDEN, OPPRESSION, AND LONELINESS

Competence has nothing to do with it. This is all about our behavior. How does overburden happen? Since we do not have a history of holding power in the public arena, it reflects our twisted belief that we must do it all – kids, husbands, professional careers, thin figures, beautiful hair, facial harmonization, libido, and so on. As if doing it all was the price to pay in exchange for our free choice. Do you see what I mean? Can you see how perverse this system is?

Here are some examples: you're married and have a job you like, but the salary is low. Then you have a child, and the scenario pressures you to quit working – after all, that money is not going to make much of a difference in the household's overall income. From that point on, your home and your child are your responsibility, and you start being treated like a housewife - as if managing a house was not work.

Then, your child grows up a bit, and you feel empty. You want to go back to work and start your own business. As it would be nearly impossible to keep a job at a company. Since you're a good baker, you decide to make and sell homemade cakes – and it goes well. There you have it: you're OVERBURDENED. Do you know why? Because you took on task after task, and no one is going to make anything easier for a woman who starts doing something on her own and begins to make money. How dare you?

To avoid being overwhelmed, you need to delegate the work: your house needs a housekeeper, and your child will need a babysitter or an extension of the school hours because YOU HAVE ANOTHER JOB! And those people will be your employees, paid with the money earned from your business. Do you get it? When you accept that you should not have to pay a toll in order to exist professionally, you can say goodbye to all the anxiety and anxiety pills you have been taking. Your health and the quality of your time as a mother, wife, friend, and professional will improve.

MYSOGYNIST OPPRESSION, on the other hand, works more subtly and ultimately sustains female overburden. Yep! It represents the power of the scenario that is hostile to women, encompassing everything that limits them: your mother saying you must be dedicated to your husband or he will find someone else; your mother-in-law badgering for another grandchild; your husband claiming that you're working too much and getting fat; your best friend who won't support your career plans; your vendor using a friendly hug as an excuse to run his hand along your back; your coworker commenting on your outfit in front of your boss; organizations that rather close big contracts with other men; the bank that denies the loan application to expand your business; the haters that attack you on the internet when you start to grow.

It's hard. It's oppressive. It is the force that defies your light and sunshine and does everything in its power to break and leave you in shambles, cornered. You won't even know how it happened.

LONELINESS is the side effect of the force exerted by oppression on your life. You are EXHAUSTED and convinced that all of that only happens to you, that you're doing something wrong, that maybe you shouldn't dare so much, that you have no team or anyone on your side to help you or to hold your hand. At the end of the day, there is only one way out: to give up any action that would take you forward and help you grow.

If you are unaware of the full scale of the perversity in the world, as described above, and fail to reverse the process, you will be a VILLAIN of your own life: a perpetual foot-dragger, a whiner, a sad and insecure person who resents successful women. I do not want that to happen, and I will not allow you, or any other woman, even myself, to go to that place again. Enough is enough! It's time we recognize this vicious cycle and break it. How? By assuming our role as a PROTAGONIST or nourishing the seed to become UNLEASHED that is inside all of us.

To begin the process, it is crucial that you have a deep knowledge of yourself and the historical context and that you stop believing that only annoying feminists fight for women's rights and that it is much ado about nothing. After I traced the three primary causes of professional bankruptcy and capitulation affecting women, I came upon a study by Sebrae Brazil that explained the nine female personas in the job market, specifying their fears, strengths, weaknesses, and reasons to build a business.

I learned from my readers that five of those nine personas were more common: TIRED, COMPETITIVE, INSECURE, INVISIBLE, and ANXIOUS.

I decided to combine fiction, which I knew very well, with the study of those personas and developed characters based on true stories for each one. I insist that if we can understand our vulnerabilities, we can leverage our strengths, and that is how we become UNLEASHED.

As a result, I present to you our fellow ladies, describing how each persona acts regarding VILLAIN behavior and the changes required to become PROTAGONISTS. This has helped countless women to identify their blind spots, bring them into the light, and to grow stronger from that awareness. Are you prepared to really look at yourself? Dear reader, before I begin the next chapter, I would like to introduce you to my partner in content development for the TRANSFORMATIVE JOURNEY OF BECOMING UNLEASHED, the amazing VIRGINIA DE GOMEZ. To make up the contents of the UNLEASHED education course, Virginia and I combined aspects of mythology, philosophy, art, and the personality enneagram, and, based on the female anguishes on the job market, we built an identification framework to outline the behavioral patterns of the five personas, which we will describe in the following pages.

For every human anguish, pleasure, fear, or need, we writers have to be open and ready to identify new archetypes and develop new characters that better represent the new woman of today. After all, who wants to read a book, watch a movie, or a soap opera that has NOT ONE character resembling the woman that you are? Or even anyone that you know?

Here, we are going to understand the modernization of today's female archetypes. Is every archetype an example of positive behavior? Are all archetypes heroic characters? Not always. An archetype is generally a neutral reference, as it is a totally human, dual model of behavior.

But what determines if you are portraying the bright or dark side of the archetype is whether you choose to listen to or ignore your "inner villain" or the "protagonist of your own story."

Each of the five personas is an invitation to reflect on what leads us to our unknowing side (which we call the VILLAIN) or to our conscious side (which we call the PROTAGONIST). Conscience triggers our strengths and talents.

PART 3

MAKE A COMMITMENT TO YOURSELF

"Do you want to make your childhood dreams come true?"

OUR FELLOW FEMALES, OUR STORIES

A. MELISSA – THE EXHAUSTED WOMAN

She is a woman who generally has children and continues to work outside the home as well. She accumulates tasks. But she feels good taking on the responsibility, besides the fact that she needs the money. Melissa's hair is constantly disheveled. She never goes to the doctor, does not care for her own health, and has completely denied herself.

What is her vulnerability? Melissa can no longer recognize herself. She looks in the mirror and vainly searches for the woman she was before she had children. This makes her feel like a failure. Easy now, that is just the EXHAUSTION and LACK OF SUPPORT talking. She can turn all that into something positive, resolving and changing those vulnerabilities into strengths. Melissa's biggest strength is her responsibility towards her family. She is a woman of a great asset within the job market, whatever the market is.

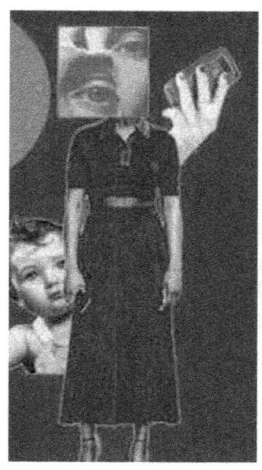

Outlining Melissa:

Anguish:

Pressured by impossible deadlines at work and in her personal life;

Compromised health;
Lacks motivation.

Fear:

Failing to do it all;
Getting sick and unable to work;
Losing her job.

Pleasure:

Meeting deadlines;
Spending time with family;
Feeling rested.

Dream:

An organized schedule;
Healthy habits (professional and personal);
Balance work and family.

The goal in starting her own business:

Free time and flexible hours.
The challenge of starting her own business:
Overcome the fear of losing what little financial security she has.

Advantages of starting her own business:

The possibility of working out of her home (or home office).

B. CLAIRE – THE COMPETITIVE WOMAN

Claire is the woman who was raised to believe that WOMEN CANNOT BE FRIENDS, which is reflective of female competition from her teen years, when she would hook up with a boy, even though she didn't really want to, just to prove to her friends that she was the hottest one in the group. When she grew up, Claire became a woman driven to win the "gold medal" in everything she did, focusing all her energy on others rather than herself. By constantly comparing herself and competing with other women, she relinquishes her authenticity and always comes in second, feeling defeated.

However, she is a powerhouse. She is brave and extremely capable, but her weakness lies in her insistence on measuring her own worth based on the achievements of those around her rather than on her own accomplishments. The neighbor's grass is always greener than hers. Additionally, she harbors resentment for the competition. Distressing, huh?

Outlining Claire:

Anguish:

    Not standing out;

    Not being promoted;

    Not being disputed on the market.

Fear:

    Being forgotten;

    Being put down;

    Not making it to the finals.

Pleasure:

    Winning;

    Taking the lead;

    Reaping the winner's benefits.

Dream:

    Earn the highest salary;

    Achieve the best results on the market;

    Be the most expensive professional on the market.

The goal in starting her own business:

    Be the entrepreneur of the year.

The challenge of starting her own business:

    Overcome her fear of not being an instant success.

Advantages of starting her own business:

    Being strategic and a fighter.

C. SOPHIA – THE INSECURE WOMAN

Most often, Sophia has some artistic talent, engaging in the arts - culinary art, fashion, or literature. Despite her talent, she is ashamed of showing it off. Her strength is the impact made by her work, and her weakness is not believing in it. Sophia is an "easy mark" for abusive men since she is always expecting someone to validate her talent. When that does not happen, she feels insecure and wronged by the world. What Sophia has yet to understand is that only she has the power to validate her creations. Otherwise, she will continue to be the same insecure woman for the rest of her life and may even give in to envy, which would destroy her.

She works here and there and pays her bills but is unable to advance toward acknowledgment and success. Her talent is hidden away in a drawer, hoping that someone (usually a male power figure) will open it and retrieve her treasure trove. Whenever "Sophia" decides to build her own business and put her work on the market employing a strategy, she succeeds and experiences the power of being a protagonist and an UNLEASHED.

Outlining Sophia:

Anguish:

    Invisibility;

    Discredit;

    Trivialization of her talents.

Fear:

    Never succeeding in showing her talents;

    Not being recognized for her abilities;

    Not doing something she loves for a living.

Pleasure:

    Offering tips on her area of expertise;

    Being hailed as a point of reference in her field;

    Creating projects in her field.

Dream:

    Be famous;

    Make money from her talents;

    Have creative freedom.

The goal in starting her own business:

    Make the most of her talents and passions.

    The challenge of starting her own business:

    Overcome her fear of not having an audience.

Advantages of starting her own business:

    Knowing her talents quite well.

D. LAURA – THE INVISIBLE WOMAN

Laura occupies the last desk at the back of the office and hides behind a computer because she does not want to be seen. Behind the desk, she is a pro who, in addition to being great with spreadsheets and management, makes sure not a cent goes to waste. The combination of these qualities is seldom found on the market since the financial area is still not one where women thrive. However, although she knows how competent she is, she chooses to hide so she won't have to take a stand. If she manages to defeat that fear of exposure, she becomes a valuable manager, working with diverse teams and an excellent mediator of conflicts.

The trigger that reinforces her vulnerability is her physical appearance. "Laura" is not outgoing and is not a typical beauty. She finds herself awkward and even ugly. It is her physical insecurity that makes her invisible. If she worked on her self-acceptance, self-worth, and self-reliance, she could solve that problem and become an amazing leader.

Outlining Laura:

Anguish:
Lacking a voice;
Lacking a purpose;
Meager prospects for the future.

Fear:
Being rejected for her physical appearance;
Failing to achieve stability;
Failing to do anything important.

Pleasure:
Getting a compliment;
Being acknowledged;
Being respected.

Dream:
Have her own team;
Be able to speak up confidently;
Secure new work opportunities.

The goal in starting her own business:
Build a business that works in her way and on her terms.

The challenge of starting her own business:
Overcome her insecurities and show herself.

Advantages of starting her own business:
Being able to plan each step calmly.

E. TONY – THE ANXIOUS WOMAN

Tony is the spitfire who is determined to do it all, who likes many things, knows a lot of people, rules social media, takes on too much, and neglects her personal life. If she's dating, she can never figure out why she can't make time for her partner. She can't take a vacation or even the weekend off to relax.

She is constantly wired. Her vulnerability lies in her need for acceptance. She can't say no. On the other hand, her strengths are competence and excellence: when she proposes to do something, there is no doubt that it will turn out better than expected.

Outlining Tony:

Anguish:

    She is very stressed out;
    She is constantly paranoid;
    She feels anxious.

Fear:

    Losing control;

    Being ridiculed;

    Failing to see a job through to completion.

Pleasure:

    Seeing a plan that she has conceived come to fruition;
    Having control over the allocation of tasks/time;
    Meeting deadlines, and honoring agreements.

Dream:

    Discover simple, effective organization methods;
    Plan out her career over the next twelve months (not have to put out fires);
    Properly balance her work and personal life.

The goal in starting her own business:

    Be her own boss.

The challenge of starting her own business:

    Overcome her professional confusion, or at least find out where to begin.

Advantages of starting her own business:

    She is fierce.

When the study with my readers was finished…

I realized I could develop a business course to prepare ENTREPRENEURS, focusing on female issues, to solve the problems posed by the VILLAIN in each of the five personas I had outlined. All of this was turned into a method, the UNLEASHED TRANSFORMATIVE JOURNEY. I found out that our feminine issues have nothing to do with competence since they are not associated with our skills and ability to study and understand things. Those issues are connected with our historical DNA because we have never been encouraged to be independent. The support for our advancement is scarce, and a woman's initiative is always treated with consternation, even if it is just a girl who decides to tell a boy she likes him. That is because when we were finally allowed to work and gain financial independence, we accessed a world built by men. That is why we often feel lonely and overburdened in our fields.

Before we solve the problems of our fellow females in each group with the UNLEASHED TRANSFORMATIVE JOURNEY, I need to talk about the collective villains who impact all women, regardless of their identity. If those villains are not stopped, we will never beat them.

Whether we hold the highest position in a company or own the best business enterprise in the world, if we act in the manner of the collective villains, everything will go awry. They are why we often see failures and frustrations instead of focusing on solving problems and achieving success. They prevent us from perceiving the power of our skills and cause us to engage in a mental struggle. Each one gives rise to the specific villains associated with the five personas.

There are seven collective villains:
1. Lack of confidence in her abilities
2. Doubts on how to see herself as her own enterprise
3. Insecurity to show her talents
4. Discouragement to change what bothers her
5. Fear of criticism and fear of making mistakes
6. Extreme urgency to make it work, which compromises the planning process
7. Procrastination to implement the plan of action and get to work.

These limiting behaviors and mental attitudes would affect anyone's performance to the extent that they prevent us from giving our best. It is not insignificant that these attitudes are imposed upon us by the INVISIBLE CLOAK of our male chauvinist, racist, homophobic society. In it, the heterosexual white male is born the lord of the land.

I am not attempting to diminish the achievements of these men but simply setting things in the proper places: opportunities and privileges are not distributed equally among everyone. Until you understand that once and for all, you will continue to collaborate with the collective villains that affect you.

The best way to handle constricting beliefs is with cognitive-behavioral therapy. Today, sessions are more accessible, and even institutions e colleges offer that kind of service free of charge. So, freeing yourself from that amount of limitation is up to you alone, and, believe me, no one is going to take you by the hand to get it done.

What's up with our fellow females?

Now that we are familiar with the collective villains, let's SOLVE OUR FELLOW FEMALES' PROBLEMS and talk about the specific villains inherent to each fellow female/ persona, so you can figure out which group you identify with. I have prepared a test to help you do that. It has ten questions: you should choose just one option for each question. Then, write down the letter that appears most among your answers and find out which is your dominant persona and how to turn your villain into a protagonist.

TEST TO IDENTIFY YOUR PERSONA

Dear reader who is on your way to becoming UNLEASHED, the following test is critical for you to embark on the transformative experience this book can provide you. There are ten questions: please choose just one option for each question. If your answers are split equally between different letters, for example, if in the end, you have five questions with an answer A and five questions with an answer B, add up the two results. The test won't work if you choose more than one option per question.

CONCERNING LEADERSHIP

- A. I believe leadership is about union, not individuality.
- B. I believe leadership is a place for winners, not women who cower in the face of problems.
- C. I believe leadership is for creative women who get deeply involved in everything they do, not for superficial or predictable people.
- D. I am a better follower than I am a leader.
- E. I believe leadership is for reasonable, reliable women who keep their word, not for deceptive people.

CONCERNING LIFE

   A. I try too hard to please everyone around me.

   B. I express optimism in light of the unexpected.

   C. I am more tolerant of losers than winners.

   D. I am more interested in my personal life than in my career.

   E. I sometimes display obedience to avoid conflicts, but ultimately do what I believe is right in my own way.

CONCERNING PLANNING

   A. I can usually plan my schedule in advance, but I can never keep it since I am constantly having to bail out someone or assist someone.

   B. I can never plan in advance because I hate the bureaucratic, overly structured part of planning.

   C. I can never plan in advance because I like to respect my own rhythm and let things flow.

   D. I can never plan in advance because I depend on other people's decisions and permissions.

   E. I can never plan in advance without imagining everything that could go wrong.

CONCERNING VALUES

   A. Among my core values are generosity, closeness, and acceptance.

   B. Among my core values are practicality, triumph, and promptness.

   C. Among my core values are talent, pleasure, and sensitivity.

D. Among my core values are modesty, impartiality, and neutrality.

E. Among my core values are reliance, prevention, and stability.

CONCERNING WOMANHOOD

A. It is best to feign friendship with other women than gain an enemy.

B. Women are so competitive that they will even fight for the position of most supportive of their fellow females.

C. Women have so often stolen my ideas, contacts, and opportunities that I prefer to work alone when it is up to me.

D. All women seem more brilliant than I am, so I always feel small in their presence.

E. I don't know to what extent I can trust other women.

CONCERNING FEAR

A. I fear not being liked by people.

B. I fear wasting time on highly bureaucratic projects or having no immediate impact.

C. I fear being anonymous, my talent going unacknowledged.

D. I fear being pressured to take the lead and make decisions.

E. I fear being betrayed during the course of my projects.

CONCERNING STRENGTH

    A. My strong suit: motivating people.

    B. My strong suit: finding shortcuts to a speedier victory.

    C. My strong suit: authenticity and passion in everything I do.

    D. My strong suit: assuaging the people on my team.

    E. My strong suit: loyalty and responsibility toward everyone who works with me.

CONCERNING WEAKNESS

    A. My weakness: I have emotional shutdowns when people I help are ungrateful.

    B. My weakness: because I am impatient, I end up not prioritizing the quality of my deliveries and later waste time redoing the work.

    C. My weakness: I need praise from others to ensure I am good at my work.

    D. My weakness: I am hesitant to take on the responsibilities of leadership.

    E. My weakness: I take on too many assignments and make a mess when delivering them.

CONCERNING PROFESSIONAL AMBITION

    A. My ambition is to be crucial to the proper functioning of my workgroup.

    B. My ambition is to achieve professional independence at my own pace without having to keep up with the other members of my team.

    C. My ambition is to be recognized as a unique, original talent for what I do.

    D. My ambition is to be an example of the proper balance between personal and professional life.

    E. My ambition is to be treated as a professional capable of solving and preventing problems.

CONCERNING ONGOING PROFESSIONAL ATTITUDES

    A. I am more mindful of other people's deadlines and goals than mine.

    B. I believe that keeping a high-stress level makes me more dexterous, challenging, and productive.

    C. I am hurt when other people do not recognize my talent and tend to self-sabotage.

    D. I make myself vulnerable so that I am neither seen nor pushed because I dislike being at the center of attention.

    E. I can only see what is wrong and what is lacking or capable of compromising the project I am working on.

PERSONA TEST RESULT

Dearest reader, your dominant persona is the option that most came up in your test. Please remember that all of us have two sides: the VILLAIN and the PROTAGONIST. The villain takes you toward victimization, procrastination, and failure. The protagonist, in turn, imbues you with strength, empowerment, and accomplishment. To make the transition, you must know both sides extremely well so that you can identify when you are under the influence of one or the other and make the right choice for the behavior that will make you UNLEASHED.

A. The tired villain

When you heed your TIRED VILLAIN side, you become the embodiment of an eager, exhausting professional, often with strong opinions/demanding, explosive behaviors.

What does the tired villain want?

- Turn every woman into an embodiment of the invasive, manipulative female character.
- The goal is to influence you to become more stagnant and insecure for believing that you get less love than others.
- The plan is to make everything so mixed up between personal and professional relationships in the workplace that the professional course ultimately becomes a perpetual little club where women compete for people's love.
- The purpose is to expose you to the market as a nosy, controlling, gossipy, brown-nosing professional.

When this villain guides your attitudes, what does that look like?

- You believe you are the most realistic of all: proving that you know everything that can go wrong is crucial. You become THE LIGHTHOUSE THAT PREDICTS THE STORM: so that you can say,"I told you so… I knew it". She makes us "tragic." You constantly prioritize mistakes and losses.
- You become rude: this villain makes us blunt and drives us to uncover every lie and falsehood. But this habit could turn into

a worn-out pattern. Being the first to start an unsanctioned investigation, to spread unverified suspicions, or to experience the adrenaline of not knowing, is critical to the TIRED VILLAIN.

- Because she feels threatened (emotionally and physically), her own distrust makes her desperate, and she will ultimately tend to believe anything.

- She is ambiguous: this villain makes us act like women who want to be seen as professionals who constantly change their minds and behaviors so that, in the end, no one knows what she thinks. Clearly unsteady in her definitions, she fuels the fantasy that she has control of the unexpected. We become anxious women, trying to anticipate everything that can go wrong while pretending that everything has been planned.

How does the market treat the tired villain?

- Like the annoying individual, she always offers what no one asks for. She is constantly shifting between eager positivity and demands for gratitude, which causes the market to be wary of her.

- Like an invasive presence: someone who always buds in and thinks she knows what's best for everyone.

- Like a manipulator: she attempts to influence other people's decisions. Always makes it clear that she can hurt someone just by "opening her mouth" to the right people. She deliriously believes that will make her appear more vital to any project, client, or deal.

What are the 3 biggest challenges imposed on you by this villain?

- Reconsider your arrogant attitude towards anyone who does not appear open to you: she becomes outraged as soon as someone sets limits on her eager disposition/inordinate interest. It is not uncommon for her to treat the person as "undeserving." Someone she wasted her precious time on and was not worth it.

- Reconsider your arrogant attitude towards anyone who does not reciprocate what you offer: the villain behaves like "the overbearing mama no one invited to the show." Later, she'll claim she can't understand why she is not praised for her advice. She feels unappreciated and gets revenge by setting little "traps" to make the person feel less than her.

- Reconsider the arrogant attitude you assume when faced with your own needs: this is a woman who goes to extremes to take care of everyone and everything so that it will appear that she does not need anything from others. She won't have to face her hidden insecurities. Her internal disconnection prevents her from recognizing and meeting her needs personally. She is always last on her list of priorities.

What are the 3 traps you should avoid falling into?

- Believing that your fate is to do everything for other people, even though you know they will be unappreciative.

- Your urge to stay connected to as many people as possible makes you feel hostage to their praise and approval so you can feel you are on the right path.

- You rarely show the same attention to the quality of your deliveries and deadlines as you do to interpersonal relationships.
- Deep down, you know you have more to give and much more to gain in life, and you deserve better than to experience just that side of yourself. When you realize any of those attitudes is guiding you, you become UNLEASHED. You are well on your way to change because the decision to do so was made by the PROTAGONIST in you to prompt immediate change.

B. The competitive villain

When you heed the advice of your COMPETITIVE VILLAIN, you become the embodiment of a professional who competes with everything and everyone over anything. She is often heavily influenced by male chauvinist, intolerant opinions and behaviors.

What does the competitive villain want?

- Turn every woman into a representation of the age-old myth of "female competitiveness."
- The goal is to drive her to grow more and more aggressive and angry about losing in any situation.
- She plans to make the professional environment so antagonistic and conflictive in her interpersonal relationships that her career ultimately becomes a perpetual battlefield and a constant struggle.
- The goal is to present you to the market as a treacherous and adversarial, poor team player.

When this villain guides your attitudes, what does that look like?

- She is calculating: being the shrewdest, always gunning for a loophole, is crucial. She forces you to be a GOLD-DIGGER: to prefer associating with those on top, leaving behind anyone who is weak or unimportant.

- She is scrappy: turning you into a "ruthless player," driving you to sabotage anyone you see as an obstacle.

- She is the first to start conflicts and animosities. Because this villain wants no competition of any kind. She is always prepared for war, even in situations where partnerships should be created.

- She is distant: makes you act like a woman who wants to be seen as an exceedingly practical, impatient, ruthless professional, and someone who is impersonal, constantly disguising her emotions and acting deliberately.

How does the market treat the competitive villain?

- Like a threat: the destruction this villain leaves in her wake cause the market to be scared of her.

- Like an imposter: someone who is capable of anything to get ahead.

- Like an "amateurish": a person who neglects the quality and effort put into her deliveries because she is already thinking about the next project, client, or deal.

What are the 3 biggest challenges imposed on you by this villain?

- Anger against other women: she is a ruthless team member, partner, or boss towards other women (especially those she considers to be losers or potential competitors). She has an uncontrollable urge to expose other women's incompetence or passivity to the world.

- Angry at having to structure the path: she behaves like someone who is constantly trying to bypass basic rules and laws. She believes being faster is more important than being disciplined and even more important than realizing what the market demands.

- Resentful of emotions: she appears to be a woman who lacks empathy and pretends to be veritably interested in the people she suspects. As a result, she misses the opportunity to connect to her true motivations and values.

What are the 3 traps you should avoid falling into?

- Believing (and actually sustaining) the idea that her fate is to constantly fight about everything.

- The unwillingness to accept life's timing (disguised as proactivity) creates a constant state of stress.

- Believing that it is hard to find good partnerships to achieve new goals.

CAUTION: expecting your professional recognition to happen through conflict and turning your work routine into a war among women is the result reaped by any woman who heeds the advice of her COMPETITIVE VILLAIN.

Deep down, you know you have more to give and much more to gain in life, and you deserve better than to experience just that side of you. When you realized any of those attitudes were guiding you, you found yourself UNLEASHED. You are well on your way to change because the decision to do so was made by the PROTAGONIST in you to prompt immediate change.

C. The insecure villain

When you heed the advice of your INSECURE VILLAIN, you become the embodiment of a temperamental, overly sensitive-professional. Strong opinions, dramatic and unexpected behaviors often drive her.

What does the insecure villain want?

- Make every woman a representation of the jealous, impassioned female.
- The goal is to make you increasingly unstable and angry for believing you are less celebrated than others.
- The plan is to make everything so bitter and murky in the workplace that your career ultimately turns into a perpetual talent show in which the loser is publicly humiliated (your biggest fear).
- The intention of this villain is to present you to the market as an unstable, contemptible professional who is jealous of everyone.

When this villain guides your attitudes, what does that look like?

- Thinks she is special: you have to prove that you are the victim of jealousy or that people are excluding you because of your genius. She is "the exotic" one: with the sole purpose of shocking the planet and proving that you are that irreverent and petulant. This villain compels you to be "egocentric," choosing to be with people by whom you don't feel threatened (even if those people ultimately take you down) and to outshine those you believe to be well-respected.

- She is petty: she drives you to target any person that you believe wants to hog the limelight.

- She is the first to initiate rivalry games and emotional manipulations. Because you feel insecure when faced with any competition, you are always defensive, feeling offended, even in situations that could be productive and creative for you.

- She feels persecuted and sabotaged: this villain leads you to act like a woman who wants to be seen as a professional who will not assume a protagonist role nor show her creativity. She turns you into a woman dependent on praise who will not adjust to anything or anyone. And whenever someone does not offer that, she sees them as her enemy.

How does the market treat the insecure villain?

- Like a snake: the deeply inquisitive eye that this villain displays fuels the market's rejection of her.

- A snob who believes she is quite special, with unique tastes and temperament. However, the market sees her as "eccentric, high maintenance, and unreasonable.
- Like a drama queen: she creates a situation over anything. She always thinks there is someone trying to take her down or steal her extremely creative projects, ideas, and clients.

What are the 3 biggest challenges imposed on you by this villain?

- Letting go of the resentment against other creative individuals: as soon as any idea receives more praise than or is approved before your own, you take it personally, making it so no one can stand being around you. You become an unpredictable team member, partner, or boss, who leaves everyone waiting to see what crazy thing you'll do next.
- Letting go of the resentment against anyone who criticizes you: you behave like "the temperamental weirdo at the company" but cannot figure out why you are not appreciated. You feel unfairly judged and believe you are being sabotaged for being unique and having such a special talent.
- Letting go of the resentment against your lukewarm life: you become a woman who pursues exhilaration, inspiration, or the meaning of life through intense and twisted paths. During the course of your chaotic pursuit, you miss opportunities to connect with the world in a truly creative, unbiased manner.

What are the 3 traps you should avoid falling into?

- Believing your fate is to have talent but not as much luck, opportunities, or recognition as other women.
- Being childish and egocentric.
- Focusing your serpent gaze: lurking in the shadows in order to push people away so that no one can knock you down.

CAUTION: do not aim to eliminate all the creative, beautiful, and interesting people around you; believing they envy you, or turning your work routine into a secretive spy game full of manipulation and resentment, can turn every decision in your life into a soap opera.

Deep down, you know you have more to give and much more to gain in life, and you deserve more than to experience just that side of you. When you realized you were being guided by some of those flaws, you found my UNLEASHED book. Now, you are well on your way to change because the PROTAGONIST made the decision to do so in you.

D. The invisible villain

When you heed the advice of the INVISIBLE VILLAIN, you become the embodiment of the anonymous professional. She is often strongly influenced by passive-aggressive behaviors and does not even know it.

What does the invisible villain want?

- They want you to be unaware of your power, leading you to believe that you are effectively powerless.

- The goal is to make you feel limited out of fear of surrendering the space you have secured, and you settle for less.
- The plan of this villain is to make the work environment so bland that your personal life gets all your attention.
- They want to present you to the market as a disinterested, procrastinating professional.

When this villain guides your attitudes, what does that look like?

- She is unassertive: she runs away and hides from confrontations, explanations, and decisions, essentially putting her life in the hands of others.
- She is discrete so as not to invite the duties inherent to her professional career.
- She is insensitive, disguising her ability to connect with other people.
- She assumes no major responsibilities toward anyone, pretending not to see the dissatisfaction of those around her, as that is the only way she can keep herself distant, accepting no blame.
- She heightens her invisibility so no one will think to call on her, as she never contributes.
- She is notoriously namby-pamby and will be seen as a powerless woman.
- She becomes half-hearted and inconsistent towards the more important things in life and society.

How does the market treat the invisible villain?

- It does not believe in her skills and treats her like a "run-of-the-mill" professional: someone in the game but no one trusts enough to pass the ball to, so she is constantly overlooked. And since she is treated with indifference, she responds with laxness and impassibility.

What are the 3 biggest challenges imposed on you by this villain?

- Overcome the reluctance to pay the price of your professional growth: you have become a woman who is seen by the world as unaccountable and believes everything is just a "big hassle."
- Overcome the reluctance to assume your protagonism: you behave like someone not interested in playing an active role in your own life and are completely unwilling to take the lead.
- Overcome the reluctance to make fast decisions: you miss out on opportunities to be recognized as a woman who impacts your family, your team, and your company. So, you become undervalued, like a person who is unresponsive to issues that others deem crucial and urgent.

What are the 3 traps you should avoid falling into?

- Believing your fate is to remain anonymous.
- Procrastinating at work.
- Failing to move towards new goals.

CAUTION: never expect your professional recognition to fall out of the sky (without conflict, effort, or antagonism); never play the victim to justify your choice to focus more energy on your personal life rather than your professional life, as this feeds the INVISIBLE VILLAIN.

Deep down, you know you have more to give and much more to gain in life, and you deserve better than to experience just that side of you. When you realize any of those attitudes is guiding you, you become UNLEASHED. You are well on your way to change because the decision to do so was made by the PROTAGONIST in you to prompt immediate change.

E. The anxious villain

When you heed the advice of the ANXIOUS VILLAIN, you may not always see it, but you will exist in a state of constant anxiety, especially because you invariably disguise your frustrations. Keep in mind that everyone notices this because you make an effort to appear motivated, with a semblance of constant exhilaration and often demanding, explosive behaviors.

What does the anxious villain want?

- The ANXIOUS VILLAIN wants to turn every woman into an embodiment of the lost, powerless female.
- Her goal is to drive you to become increasingly cowardly and submissive for believing that you have less emotional stability than others.
- The plan of this villain is that, in your workplace, things happen with such immediateness that they make the relationships ever-changing, leading you to believe that the professional environment is a dead-end, deceitful place.

- The purpose is to present you to the market as an unstable professional who fluctuates between trusting something completely and trusting nothing at all.

When this villain guides your attitudes, what does that look like?

- You believe you are the most realistic of all. You become "tragic," constantly highlighting mistakes and losses, somewhat of a "lighthouse that predicts the storm," just so you can say, "I told you so… I knew it."
- You become rude: this villain makes us "blunt" and drives us to uncover every lie and falsehood. She is the first to start an unsanctioned investigation and to spread unverified suspicions.
- She is suspicious of everything and everyone: constantly feeling threatened (both emotionally and physically). She's in despair and believes anything that she is told.
- She is ambiguous: this villain makes us act like women who want to be seen as professionals who constantly change their minds and behaviors. In the end, no one really knows what she thinks. Clearly unsteady in her definitions, she fuels the fantasy that she has control of the unexpected, trying to anticipate every single thing that can go wrong. If any institution/individual demands proof of her suspicions (raised without evidence), she becomes even more suspicious.

How does the market treat the anxious villain?

- Like a jinx: certain market niches are often quite superstitious, and constantly attempting to prove that you had predicted a problem triggers insecurity and annoys the market.
- Like a nuisance: someone always playing the devil's advocate to expose the proposed solutions and dismantle the group.
- Like a pushover: she always uses her weakness and bad luck as justifications for not assuming her protagonism.

What are the 3 biggest challenges imposed on you by this villain?

- Getting over the fear of being double-crossed/damaged: the fear of suffering any kind of loss makes her unsure about what is best at the moment. But her reluctance to make decisions brings her even more losses.
- Getting over the reluctance to waste time: she is always starting things she will not finish because she believes the next step will be more important than the present one.
- Getting over the reluctance to stop guessing: she is a woman who wastes time trying to guess every future step, which immobilizes her in the present.

What are the 3 traps you should avoid falling into?

- Believing that your fate is to be perpetually tormented about your future.
- The anguish she feels between trusting and mistrusting too much makes her insecure about her own judgment.

- Not being as loyal to yourself as you are to those you choose to trust.

CAUTION: do not aim to eliminate all the creative, beautiful, and interesting people, believing that everyone envies you. Turning your work routine into a secretive spy game, full of manipulation and resentment, can turn every decision in your life into a soap opera.

Deep down, you know you have more to give and much more to gain in life, and you deserve better than to experience just that side of you. When you realize any of those attitudes is guiding you, you become UNLEASHED. You are well on your way to change because the decision to do so was made by the PROTAGONIST in you to prompt immediate change.

LEARNING TO BE A PROTAGONIST

HOW CAN YOUR VULNERABILITY BECOME YOUR STRENGTH?

Now you already know the persona you identify with and your vulnerabilities. It is time to find out how to become the protagonist of your life, eliminating your inner villain.

A. The shift from TIRED to PROTAGONIST

When you listen to the PROTAGONIST in you, you stop being the woman who is TIRED of trying to please others and become a PARTNER. We grow into professionals who are aware of our actual, specific relevance in each situation. We find more pleasure in our journey to make life happier and surrounded by friends.

What does the protagonist want?

- Self-command: the goal is that she develops the inner strength that leads to personal control in situations where she feels slighted/ excluded. Why waste time with unnecessary emotional outbursts?

- Self-motivation: the plan is to make the work environment so stimulating and congenial that this passes on to her personal life without overburdening her. It is crucial for a PROTAGONIST to feel engaged both personally and professionally. This way, she ensures she will have strength even in times when she feels a lack of support.

- Self-knowledge: instead of aiming to please everyone.

- Excellence: the goal is to present herself to the market as a professional that has been stripped of her insecurities and anxieties since she knows exactly what she needs in order to feel RESTED and willing to turn the tables in her life. Why waste time acting like an exhausted professional constantly pretending that everything is under control?

When the protagonist guides your attitudes, what does that look like?

- Social influence: we establish relationships and partnerships and get rid of antagonisms. This is because of the ability to observe and connect the dots easily.

- The protagonist directs us to be powerful in order to stay effectively connected to people and circumstances that could open new doors and leverage the efficiency of our network.

- Efficiency without collusion: the true value lies in your ability to uplift even the most pessimistic. This gift of inspiring people with your genuine desire to help them is more valuable than any collusion employed to attract the attention of the powerful. The PROTAGONIST knows that flashing a big, empathetic smile is a good remedy against people's suspicions and reluctance.

- Sense of importance and maturity: she knows the emotional exhaustion that results from being seen as a professional who fluctuates between happy-go-lucky and someone who demands acknowledgment for her contributions. She knows how crucial it is to stay in contact with her point of awareness, which helps her not lose herself in trying to keep up with others. She is also conscious of the power of her contributions to the world and to the lives of those who choose to join her.

How does the market treat the protagonist?

- As being approachable: in many areas, the existence of a professional capable of supporting without judgment and who is approachable is very important. She is treated as an "inspiring" professional who is in the game to show how to not let your vitality and good disposition be affected by minor day-to-day interpersonal frustrations.
- As being crucial: she knows her value. As a result, the market makes concessions for her desire to be genuinely involved. And it even supports her fight for the right to value her time and energy instead of expecting validation.
- Emotional connection: she becomes a professional who is seen by the world as connected to her inner strength, which could make her exceedingly successful.

What are the biggest advantages of listening to the protagonist in you?

- Emotional connection: she becomes a professional who is seen by the world as connected to her inner strength, which could make her exceedingly successful, even if she does seem exceedingly warm.
- Time: knowing how to control her schedule so that her professional life does not consume her soul. She finds more time outside business hours to relax, recharge and go back in ready to help people manage their time.
- Genuine good disposition: what the VILLAIN does purely out of arrogance, the PROTAGONIST does with kindness. She is no longer interested in rubbing anyone's face about how she

carries the weight of the world on her back. After all, she makes a point of staying connected so that her sense of belonging remains current. She is free to spend time with whomever she chooses to do so.

What are the 3 major motivations that every protagonist must practice?

- Self-discipline.
- Her work threshold.
- Controlling her own schedule, reserving time to rest.

What are the 3 core beliefs that all protagonist share?

- The belief that your fate is to forge bonds, attend to and leverage the team/company like no other professional.
- The belief that keeping control of your time and managing more people at once relieves you from having to chase after everyone like crazy or feeling overburdened (while pretending that everything is fine).
- The belief that investing in comfort, financial security, and time for yourself ensures real energy and enthusiasm.

CAUTION: never be dependent on other people; do not do everything for others; thinking about yourself first is not selfish; remember to put on your oxygen mask first before helping others.

Ideal fields: all that you want, as long as you are rested and organized.

B. The shift from COMPETITIVE to PROTAGONIST

When you heed the PROTAGONIST's counsel, you shift from COMPETITIVE to WINNER. Under the influence of your protagonism, you become a professional who does not fear competition because you know what makes you unique, who to associate with, and how and when to win. You become more transparent and truthful, and life grows more productive and dynamic.

What does the protagonist want?

- Assertiveness: the goal is to be more and more truthful about what you want, which is to win. Do not disguise your intentions. Focus on them with the same intensity, and do not feel bad for wanting to win.

- Proactivity: the plan is that the work environment establishes clear values for everyone. Do not allow your team to believe you want A when you really want B.

- Coordination: the purpose is to present yourself to the market as a professional who can manage her own desires while at the same time bargaining with the desires of others. That requires you to be mindful of your competitive instincts and control them. Make room for your bargaining instincts, combining the two sides into something that will be positive for everyone. That will prevent you from becoming the difficult or slick person who thinks no one can see your tricks. Empowering your bargaining skills will position you as the professional who makes progress for everyone involved.

When the protagonist guides your attitudes, what does that look like?

- Quick results: staying motivated is crucial so she will not disconnect from the goal. Small but constant results could help to stay the course longer. She is "alert" and effectively connected to the people and circumstances that streamline her life without the pressure of always having to be the canniest.

- High impact: here, the value lies in your observation skills to determine which issue is most capable of quickly opening doors. The PROTAGONIST knows that giving the market what it wants is the best remedy to facilitate and expedite her entry into wherever she wants.

- Gold medal: since the PROTAGONIST knows how frustrating it is to lose the game, she also understands how important it is to give out medals of encouragement to all the people involved in an issue (whether personal or professional). This keeps them committed to the group's success. The PROTAGONIST knows this reinforces her image as an intelligent, strategic, capable woman and inspires those lucky enough to be on her team.

How does the market treat the protagonist?

- The market treats her as a woman of vision, a winner who holds the solutions to the more complex issues and is not afraid to make hard decisions. In addition, the market knows that you are capable of closing deals with competitors or adversaries due to your admirable negotiating skills.

What are the 3 biggest advantages of listening to the protagonist in you?

- You always have time for you: your reputation as quick and on-point eliminates the concern that time will be wasted during the course of the negotiations.
- You are treated as a professional who can "put out fires": someone who goes into the game to show others how to change course in light of pressure or the unexpected quickly. She is truly priceless.
- Independence: because she is a professional who does not want to come in last, she has control of her time to allocate it as she finds best.

What are the 3 major motivations that every protagonist must practice?

- Agility: to become a woman who is seen by the world as an extremely ambitious professional who knows exactly what she is doing, averting the creation of new obstacles.
- Rationality: to behave like a woman capable of detachedly examining who can contribute to her advancement in the medium and long term without the limitations of a short-sighted approach.
- Ambition: the PROTAGONIST is motivated by her competence and not by the number of people she brings down. After all, she is focused on the value of her energy and is not interested in wasting time eluding unnecessary enemies made out of immediatist ploys.

What are the 3 core beliefs that all protagonist share?

- Her fate is to leverage sales, penetrate new markets, and advance relationships/processes.
- Keeping firm control of her production pace prevents loose ends upon delivery.
- Investing in her financial control allows her to always have a cash reserve to start new projects (she loves new challenges).

CAUTION: do not feel threatened by other women; do not take other people's time for granted; make your professional routine so fluid that it works rhythmically and ensures outcomes that prove that she's a winner.

Ideal professional areas: aptitude for challenging jobs or occupations which afford her merit or prominence, such as management, corporate presidency, consulting, finance, corporate speaking, business administration in general, public speaker, actress, salesperson, and public relations.

C. The shift from INSECURE to PROTAGONIST

When you listen to the PROTAGONIST in you, you shift from being INSECURE to being TALENTED. Under the influence of your protagonism, you become a professional who understands the unique personal, professional, and social impact that she causes. You find more pleasure in making life deeper, more creative, and more significant.

What does the protagonist want?

Assertiveness: the goal is to be more and more transparent regarding your values and motivations to advance your personal and professional processes. The clearer you are, the easier it will be to solve any issues. Why waste time disguising your motivations?

Proactivity: the plan is that the professional environment is so deeply motivated (with consistent results) that the sense of prosperity will counteract any feelings of rivalry for fear of failure and hardship. What is the sense of creating a hectic environment where every person is on their own?

Coordination: the purpose is to present yourself to the market as a professional who circulates well among various groups and niches to do business. So, the PROTAGONIST does not allow herself to act like a member of the "separatist clubhouse"; she will prove she knows how to blend with diversity. After all, why waste time behaving like a professional with difficulty relating to people?

When the protagonist guides your attitudes, what does that look like?

Subjectivity: you grow increasingly sensitive to the intangible, the unknown, and the valuable in life. The more open you are to the subtleties of the world, the more inspired and inspiring you become to yourself and other women. Why waste energy comparing yourself to obvious, predictable things?

Authenticity: if the professional environment is genuine in its goals and solutions, it will also become a reflection of your personal life because the DNA of a PROTAGONIST has to be in everything that she does.

Excellence: you present yourself to the market as a professional who is involved and sensitive enough to understand what is requested and execute it with your style, exceeding expectations.

After all, why waste time behaving like a professional, constantly comparing herself to everyone?

How does the market treat the protagonist?

The market treats the TALENTED protagonist professional as unique, original, and inventive. She is treated like a sensitive person whose individual work impacts the collective.

What are the 3 biggest advantages of listening to the protagonist in you?

Intuition: In this mode, it is like seeing a ray of light in an otherwise murky situation. But, rather than relying on "personal opinions," the PROTAGONIST resorts to her own experience to determine, directly, clearly, and immediately, the best path to take. The important thing for a PROTAGONIST is knowing how to use her intuition in order to stay connected to her innermost aspirations, perceptions, and understandings, considering what the scenario presents.

Sense and purpose: here, the value lies in your deep connection to your inner greatness so that you will not lose sight of the fact that every talent and competency of yours is meant to serve a bigger purpose. The PROTAGONIST inspires us to fulfill our destiny, making our lives more legitimate. The PROTAGONIST directs you to be "unique." After all, you know what you are capable of and do not feel the need to compare yourself to anyone or anything. That is the only way you can stay creative (even in the midst of the storm).

Parity: because she knows how terrible it is to not feel seen or fully appreciated for her talents, the PROTAGONIST understands how important it is to support other underappreciated individuals and help them pick up the pieces and feel safe to express their abilities authentically without feeling less than the value placed by the market on proficient, conventional professionals. You realize that this reinforces your image as a compassionate, special, inspiring woman. And a woman who is aware of her original, enterprising potential.

What are the 3 major motivations that every protagonist must practice?

Subjective viewpoint: to become a professional who is seen by the world as someone who can see further than most people, even if she does appear odd or mysterious.

Real emotion: knowing that emotion unites and motivates, she engages the group to the point of involvement, touching on the emotional connection between their personal and professional goals.

Sophistication: what the VILLAIN does only out of envy, the PROTAGONIST does with sensitivity and intelligence. She is not burdened by unfounded paranoia, nor does she lose herself in comparisons that would only put her down. After all, she must stay connected so that her sense of competence remains current, constantly pursuing new, sophisticated developments.

What are the 3 core beliefs that all protagonist share?

Her destiny is to contribute depth, intensity, and creativity to her team/company like no other professional.

Keeping control of the time she dedicates to her career will provide her with freedom and creative leisure when she needs it.

Investing in art, pleasure, and sophisticated tastes brings inspiration and good emotional health.

CAUTION: feel inspired rather than threatened by other women's talents; don't give up when the recognition of your talents takes longer than expected; make your professional routine so bold and creative that it works instinctively, and the outcomes prove your unique talents.

Ideal professional areas: arts in general; any creative activity.

D. The shift from INVISIBLE to PROTAGONIST

When you listen to the PROTAGONIST in you, you shift from being INVISIBLE to being DIPLOMATIC. Under the influence of your protagonism, you become a professional who knows where her power lies, and you learn to better balance your life.

What does the protagonist want?

To take it easy: the goal is to grow more and more solid in your decision-making and to attain the clarity to plan your personal and professional growth. Why waste time hiding your brilliance and your talents?

To be impartial: the plan is that your professional environment will be so friendly that your personal life will not be overburdened by a shortage of time. What sense is there in creating such an impersonal environment that you feel isolated?

To be modest: the intention is to present yourself to the market as a professional who understands her contributions but does not require applause or consent to work on what she knows is important. After all, why waste time behaving like a professional with participation and integration issues?

When the protagonist guides your attitudes, what does that look like?

Sensibility: she remains lucid and reasonable concerning how, when, and where to stay silent or take a stand, which allows you not to feel pressured.

Serenity: she keeps her inner peace, so you have control of your deadlines and outcomes.

Parity: because you know the feeling of not having your potential recognized, you understand how important it is to open up space and allow for the participation of as many people on your team as possible. You grow fairer, more discrete and remarkable, and a better integrator of people.

How does the market treat the protagonist?

The market treats the DIPLOMATIC protagonist professional with the utmost respect because it understands that she can solve serious crises through her negotiation power and her unique empathy. She is also treated as reliable and assigned financial responsibilities.

What are the 3 biggest advantages of listening to the protagonist in you?

Earning respect: a professional who is capable of staying calm during a crisis is extremely valuable.

Earning the status of a wise professional: someone who is in the game to show people how to control their emotions and not be infected by collective despair.

Being trustworthy: you become a professional who does not want to take the spotlight from anyone and does not believe in exposing someone who confided secrets in her.

What are the 3 major motivations that every protagonist must practice?

Consistency: to become a woman seen by the world as a professional who knows exactly what she is doing, even if she appears shy or timid.

Maturity: to behave like a woman who is capable of taking on and performing duties and responsibilities without apathy or disinterest.

Organization: to deliver her work on time, even if you have a multitude of ideas.

What are the 3 core beliefs that all protagonist share?

The belief that your destiny is to appease and institute diversity into the team.

The belief that it is important to keep control of your work hours so that your personal life is not an escape from pressure and boredom.

The belief that investing in your physical and mental well-being ensures a better balance between your professional and personal life. It is important to care for your health.

CAUTION: you do not need other people's consent for anything; do not play the victim when you choose to remain discrete; make your professional routine pleasant; believe that your results are proof of your personal brilliance.

Ideal professional areas: human resources, social work, yoga/meditation, psychoanalysis, psychotherapy, mediation, merger management, and diplomatic work. This is not to say that they would not be successful in other areas, but they should, preferably, work for a cause or serve a purpose.

E. The shift from ANXIOUS to PROTAGONIST

When you listen to the PROTAGONIST in you, you stop being the ANXIOUS woman who constantly tries to anticipate every problem and become the BRAVE woman who trusts her decisions and strategy. Under the influence of your protagonism, you shift into a professional who is conscious of her good planning skills and vision of the future. You consolidate the mission of building a consistent, manageable future.

What does the protagonist want?

To know your limitations to keep up the excellence of your work. After all, you will never again be the person who misses deadlines for lack of planning.

To have the courage to say no to demands that cannot help you grow and will only be a waste of your time. The demands where everyone wins, except you.

To stipulate the conditions for your involvement in a project: compensation? Purpose? Novelty? Which will it be?

When the protagonist guides your attitudes, what does that look like?

Chain of command: there is no confusion about what should be done first or whom to ask for help. The ranking of priorities is based on the valuation of her own opinion about what is most relevant in the short, medium, and long terms. The BRAVE PROTAGONIST drives you to be "loyal" (to the promises made to yourself and, especially, to others) so you don't introduce disarray and instability into your vision of the future. She is committed (to herself and the situation) to seeing her goals through.

Objective analysis: your ability to create and monitor projects and goals is the true value. This gift of assessing all sides of a situation to decide on the possibilities is valuable. You know that delivering good short- and medium-term planning to the market is an excellent remedy to counteract the fear of mistakes.

Transparency: because you understand how dreadful it is not knowing who to trust, you realize the importance of offering corroboration and assurances to as many people involved in an issue as possible (whether personal or professional). The most important thing to you is making the world around you more transparent, with clear leadership criteria. You know this reinforces your image as a consistent, reliable woman. You also know the power of your "estimates" about the world and the lives of those lucky enough to join you.

How does the market treat the protagonist?

As insightful: a professional who can aptly review plans without losing control of the activities during a crisis is extremely valuable.

As a "visionary": someone who is in the game to show the team how to keep their vision of the future and develop solid arguments even when there is still no evidence to support their proposition to the market.

As a candidate for positions of trust: a professional who is not interested in robbing anyone's leadership and will not do anything to cast doubt on her projections for the future.

What are the 3 biggest advantages of listening to the protagonist in you?

Strength: to become a woman seen by the world as a professional who, even though she appears argumentative, knows who to listen to and whose advice to follow without letting it affect her performance.

Structure: to present herself as a woman who is capable of taking on and carrying out duties and responsibilities without fear, discontent, or skipping steps.

Reflection: what the VILLAIN does only solely out of insecurity is done here after it has been tested and examined by the PROTAGONIST. After all, you stay alert in order to learn, by practice, what works and what does not, now and in the future that you envision. So, you are not concerned that you could be incapable of dealing with urgent adjustments or unexpected changes.

What are the 3 major motivations that every protagonist must practice?

Believing that your destiny is to produce evidence, projections, and preventions for your team like no other professional.

Remaining in control of the time you dedicate to your career to avoid the stress of constantly thinking that you may have left a gap in one of the stages of your personal or professional projects.

Learning how to say no.

What are the 3 core beliefs that all protagonist share?

Vision: you develop an "eagle eye" for risk assessments so that you can quickly identify what is worth looking more closely at during a personal or professional examination. Why waste time struggling with incomplete data?

Prevention: making the professional environment so consistent and well-planned that any angst about your personal future is counteracted; ensuring focus and support even at times when you feel bombarded by contradictory facts.

Self-reliance: presenting yourself to the market as a professional who has secured data and analyses to understand what is asked of you and execute everything competently. After all, why waste time behaving like a professional who has trouble seeing things through?

CAUTION: invest in solid, long-term projects which involve preventive actions and protections for yourself and the world.

Ideal professional areas: digital marketing, IT, engineering, project leadership, event production, film production, and execution of major events.

Now that you're beginning to grasp your own identity as a woman let's take a moment to reflect on who you were as a child. I know the expression "childhood dreams" can sound a little cliché, lame and melodramatic, but I think we have to respect that, which is anything that you have read or seen countless times and has not lost its original meaning. So, I would like to revisit the original meaning of child.

When you were a young girl, the neutering began right after you took your first steps. That's the norm. Your parents didn't do it on purpose. They were conditioned, culturally, to rear girls in a certain way: don't hurt yourself so you don't mark your body, don't jump off the jungle gym so you don't get your dress dirty, don't laugh too loud so you don't call too much attention to yourself, don't hook up with all the guys in your class so you don't get a reputation. There were so many "don't do that" to dictate an appropriate behavior that you ultimately lost sight of your essence, that originality that makes you happy because it makes you feel like who you really are.

You might be the type of girl who fought all that, but even so, they managed to put you in a box. That's normal. I will not accept that you spend another minute away from that spontaneous, vital girl who is locked inside you. In that girl's will, your "making it," your original talent, resides. You will find what you were meant to do and give to the world there.

Try to remember: were you timid, expansive, or mischievous? What did you like to do? Did you like to play? Of all the child games, what was your favorite? What made such sense to you that nothing else mattered? Do you remember? So, it's easy, right? It is that memory that you have to cling to and understand. If you have an older aunt or a grandmother, ask them to tell you stories about your childhood and pay attention: your essence is lost in there.

That girl had a dream, which could be anything: making dresses, fixing phones, piloting airplanes, making shoes, planting trees, caring for animals, cooking, dancing, painting, roller-skating in dangerous places, pulling off the leg of a doll so you could fix it, or cutting her hair, and so much more. You will find the answer, and your heart will click when you do. From there on out, your insecurities will grow smaller, courage will take the lead in your decision-making, and you will have no more doubt about your path, even if they call you crazy.

You will have to overcome the opposing force that will arise against you, which is as powerful as your joy. That force is other people's need to control us, and it is part of the game. It is up to you to be firm, to prove that you are determined and will allow no one to belittle you!

If you must step away from some people who are close to you, it will hurt but know that when your plan starts to work out, everything will pass, and no one will talk about it again. On the contrary, everyone will say how much they supported you. Speaking of support, at times of hard decisions, changes, and making dreams come true, the real support will come from people who are not close to you, who have seen your potential without preconceptions blocking their view. Accept their help and understand you do not have to be everyone's best friend. The goal is to be a good and reliable teammate.

You will also feel lonely. But that feeling is not new. How many times has that girl felt lonely or even excluded, but she got back into the game anyway? Children are incredibly resilient. You must revisit that inner quality. Don't take solitude personally. Take it professionally. Your life is being put on the right track, and no one else can do that for you. It is a solitary process, even if you are married.

On the other hand, people who are at the same turning point will cross your path. You can learn a lot from them, especially how to detach yourself emotionally from the things that happen without feeling that everything is a big conspiracy against you. A group of UNLEASHED women will support you, help you with anything you need, and make your dream come true. The more you commit to this route change in pursuit of your happiness, the more respect you will command from everyone, even the people who are jealous of you. You will attract envy, but you only need to know that those people just wish they were in your place. Do not hold on to anger for too long. Detach yourself.

My experience learning from and teaching so many women has shown me that there are three ways to reconnect to your childhood dreams:

1. Through your childhood memories.
2. Through the assurance that generates.
3. Through the power of accomplishment that arises within you.

Even if you had a tough childhood with family problems, you were a child and surely had the opportunity to make up your favorite games to ease your pain. Your essence lies precisely in those games and not in the arguments that you may have witnessed.

The tenacity it generates is the goal in allowing yourself to be guided by your childhood dream. You will be much less likely to give up, and way more resilient to the blows to come, and even manage to avoid them because you will be connected to your truth.

The strongest motivation to heed the call of your DREAM is to connect to your essence, to that thing that you must do, or you won't be able to breathe. Your childhood dreams have that power. That will bring you more stamina and make you more assertive in your choices. Believe it!

In any case, you must be mindful of the three killers of dreams, which are:

1. The domesticating force that opposes the dream, the notorious "that is not how life works".
2. The chauvinist box they will try to fit you into, the notorious: "You don't have time to play around anymore. A woman without a man is not as appreciated!"
3. Your desire to be like everyone else, the famous "being different is a lot of work."

For me, there are three things that always keep me connected to my DREAMS:

1. Replying: that is not how life works for who? And having as references women who achieved what you want.
2. Asking myself: what is the need to always have a boyfriend, or a husband, or anyone by your side who does not support your dreams?
3. Surrounding myself with people who do not want to be like everyone else so that I can feed on authenticity.

Having a firm determination to resume the journey of your DREAM is the only way to feel more:

1. Confident.
2. Authentic.
3. Brave.

The benefit of the following the path of your dream is that you will build something that is yours, a path chosen on the basis of your beliefs and truths, without making concessions to please other people, except for your inner child. In fact, you should rearrange pictures of yourself from when you were little throughout your house. That will help you stay connected to her. Brazilian singer Marina Lima says: "Now go find out what you truly love… And the world can be yours."

This book was written to make it easier for you to resume your original journey, which is your childhood dream, and, by doing so, to contribute to your empowerment to become UNLEASHED. My dream is that women feel comfortable talking freely about money, love, careers, family, and health without judging one another, criticizing each other, or disputing who has the best little life.

Have your own life! If you believe that a husband and kids fit into it, great. More power to you. But you must remain conscious, alert, and awake, never forgetting that your decision to become YOUR OWN WOMAN is the first step.

Impediments such as not having money, being too old, or not having enough education are obsolete and can no longer be sustained. Now is the time to decide what new things are going to drive your life. You are free to update all of your goals and pursue new dreams. Do it! Create new business! Have fun with people who respect you! Aim to accomplish more.

A wonderful phrase by Nietzsche is perfectly appropriate for any UNLEASHED: "No price is too high to pay for the privilege of owning yourself."

The value of your childhood dreams is that they are key to allowing you to become what you have always had the talent and the vocation to be. Remember how you felt when you let your imagination run wild… You could be a queen, an archeologist, or bake the most delicious cakes. You could do anything! The lack of faith, the behavior control, and the cultural rules may have sullied your dreams, but they were not killed, and keeping them alive during the hardest moments is crucial for you to achieve complete independence: financial, behavioral independence, and free thinking.

You already know everything that can make you more confident and help you to become UNLEASHED.

Set more ambitious goals

Act more freely

Practice free thinking

In the end, what matters is you. So, respect and improve how you act, and support other women who don't have your knowledge and experience. Try to connect with people who have had different experiences and can share them with you. Share your talents and skills with the world. Everyone is deserving, and you deserve more.

Dear reader, thank you for reading and for your trust. I admire and applaud your courage and the person you are (becoming).

NOW IT IS YOUR TURN

The UNLEASHED TRANSFORMATIVE JOURNEY will never be a lonely path. The "Dona de Si" Institute will always be available to support you, even though it is an individual transformation process since each woman who joins us has her own story, her own subjectivity, and desires. So, the first step must be taken by each woman individually, consisting of committing to herself.

Next, I present you with a Contract, which will help you to establish that commitment to get out of the box in which patriarchal society insists on confining you and assuming the responsibility for your existence. After you do, the institute, other UNLEASHED women and I will be waiting on the outside to support you, with our groups set up on WhatsApp and Telegram, with e-mails, and with the UNLEASHED TRANSFORMATIVE JOURNEY.

Pay close attention: from this point on, the UNLEASHED seed has started to germinate within you, and your sole purpose now is to nurture it so that it grows and transforms you into the best version of yourself.

You will feel the changes in your actions as you say goodbye to the villain who refuses to believe in you and take on the PROTAGONIST role, who does not require validation from anyone in order to build her own path. That is, a happy, confident woman who is proud of the path she is building, who does not self-sabotage but rather gets to work and sees it done. A woman who experiments with herself takes chances and knows what she wants to achieve.

At last, it is time for you to sign a contract with yourself. Welcome to the best version of yourself!

COMMITMENT CONTRACT WITH MYSELF

On the one side, hereinafter referred to as CONTRACTING PARTY,

_____

_____, residing at _____, I.D. number _____, hereinafter referred to as UNLEASHED.

On the other side, hereinafter referred to as CONTRACTOR, _____, residing at _____
I.D. number _____, represented herein by its managing partner, _____, residing and domiciled at _____

SECTION 01

The purpose of this contract is the realization of the dream of _____
_____, referred to as REAL DREAM by the CONTRACTOR.

SECTION 02 – PURPOSE AND GOALS

The realization of the REAL DREAM by the CONTRACTOR will be driven by the purpose of _____, organized by the following goals: _____

SECTION 03 – EMOTIONAL ASSURANCE

The CONTRACTING PARTY undertakes to provide the CONTRACTOR with therapeutic assistance and all the additional qualifications required to bring about the DREAM. The three most important are: _____

SECTION 04 – PRACTICE

The CONTRACTING PARTY undertakes to make available to the CONTRACTOR a weekly plan of action to enable the achievement of the DREAM, to be produced every week on_____ and executed on _____

SECTION 05 – ASSISTANCE

The CONTRACTING PARTY requests the assistance of the persons most knowledgeable on any given matter and prevents the CONTRACTOR from acting on impulse. Always prefer the following individuals: _____

SECTION 06 – ENERGY DRAINS

The CONTRACTING PARTY undertakes to implement the following strategy:_____

to enable the CONTRACTING PARTY to stay away from the following people who drain her energy: _____

SECTION 07 – STRENGTHS

The CONTRACTING PARTY undertakes to leverage the following strengths of the CONTRACTOR: _____, doing the following in order to accomplish that: _____

SECTION 08 – PERSONAL WEAKNESSES

The CONTRACTING PARTY undertakes to tend to and never neglect the following weaknesses of the CONTRACTOR: _____, doing the following to help her overcome them: _____

CONTRACTING PARTY   CONTRACTOR   WITNESS 1

PART 4

MEET SOME OF OUR UNLEASHED WOMEN

1. SAMIRA RAMALHO, 32 – Teresina/PI (formerly a tired woman). She found support and an exciting network.

"After the "DONA DE SI" TRANSFORMATIVE JOURNEY, everything changed in my life, and, most importantly: I changed in my core. My confidence and self-esteem improved. I dusted off an old dream of mine that I had actually forgotten about, which was to make films. I was super committed to that; ever since, I have not stopped producing. I have tried my luck at a number of public notices and established important partnerships with artists. I have never again doubted myself or passed up opportunities for fear of not being qualified. I dramatically changed my profession, and now, I work with something that brings me tremendous joy, pleasure, and excitement. I am certain that I will be successful. Before, I worked in other fields that gave me no financial return, as I would like, or validation. I did not have the support that the "Dona de Si" Institute provides, not only to me but also to my colleagues who took the journey with me so that we could advance. The network we built has been crucial."

2. ANGÉLICA RODRIGUES, 32 – Curitiba/PR (formerly a competitive woman). She found her inner power and strengthened her power of action without having to compare herself to others.

"I am an advertiser, producer, and screenwriter. Last year, I had the excellent opportunity to enjoy a week of mentoring with Suzi Pires at the "Dona de Si" Institute, and that changed not only my professional path but especially my path to becoming a creative woman. Suzi is extremely committed to helping us – enterprising, creative, professional women – embark on our personal journeys, dreams, and hopes. And that imbued me with tremendous inner power. I had already started this process of self-awareness, of seeking my essence as a woman, and the universe conspired to give me the opportunity to get to know the institute and see up close Suzi's passion for this cause that benefits women. So, everything I experienced and learned there has surely made me stronger and helped me see the intense creative potential inside me. The "Dona de Si" Institute qualified me and greatly encouraged me to make that energy more powerful, pushing me to make assertive choices throughout my journey."

3. CLÁUDIA ROBERTA, 35 – Campo Grande/MS (formerly an insecure woman). She found inner balance and fulfillment when believing in her talent.

"Six months after everything happened, I can safely say that a lot has changed, especially in my core. Before the journey, I felt out of sorts; something was out-of-balance in my life. I searched for something but had no idea what, and I had an unshakeable feeling that something was missing. It was as if I were a car attempting to start but failing over and over. This was my life. After all the experiences of the "DONA DE SI" TRANSFORMATIVE JOURNEY at the institute, which were deep and amazing, I managed to jump-start my life, and today, I feel much more like my own woman, I feel like I own my truth, my art, my history, my life."

4. MIRTES SANTANA, 22 – São Paulo/SP (formerly an invisible woman). She developed skills that allowed her to execute her ideas, drawing on all her courage.

"I am a screenwriter and had the "DONA DE SI" experience with Suzana Pires a while back. Since then, some really cool and important things happened. I believe this was only possible because of the career action plan, which is part of the institute's program. I have developed skills to be able to execute my ideas. As a result, I ended up winning a contest that awarded a trip to Los Angeles, California, where I met professionals in the film industry, watched master classes on the U.S. industry, and even had the opportunity to pitch for a documentary project, which brought some cool developments. Boosting my self-reliance and courage was also really important for me in terms of my experiences at the institute because, as of that experience, I revisited a bunch of old ideas that I could develop. Naturally, during the journey, there were obstacles that I had to face, but even so, I realized I had a strong, loud voice inside me that I needed to let out and that the way to do that was through my scripts. My biggest acquisition from the journey was the courage to raise my voice."

5. ANA CELIA COSTA, 36 – Manaus/AM (formerly an anxious woman). She managed to learn planning and focus, earning excellent results.

"The mentoring program with Suzana Pires usually lasts just one week, but I actually consult and rely on the "Dona de Si" Institute to this day in everything I do. I studied film at "Academia Internacional de Cinema," in São Paulo – and it was amazing. I was one of the screenwriters and the director of the film "Fala com meu chefe" – in fact, I was the only woman on the team, it is worth noting. After this experience, I moved to São Paulo, attended "Academia Internacional de Cinema" and, today, I work with the audiovisual and digital markets, accomplishing more and more every day and planning my life accordingly; I left behind all the confusion from the lack of focus and planning."

ABOUT THE AUTHOR

Suzana Pires is an award-winning Brazilian actress, executive producer, and entrepreneur. Over the span of three decades, she starred in dozens of films, TV series, and plays. The first Brazilian writer to attend and graduate from the prestigious Sundance Directors Lab, Suzana broke the nation's gender barrier by becoming the first lead actress turned head writer and showrunner.

Unleashed, a Latina's guide to uncover her inner power is about women's empowerment as a way for women everywhere to advocate and bring awareness to feminism and female empowerment amongst Latinas. The focus is to neutralize women's three greatest pains through personal development: work overload, oppression, and loneliness.

Through her foundation and book *Unleashed*, she is furthering the message of women's empowerment worldwide.

BIBLIOGRAPHY

MYTHOLOGY:

CAMPBELL, Joseph. The Power of Myth – Goddesses: mysteries of the feminine divine. São Paulo: Palas Athena, 1992.

BRANDÃO, JUNITO DE SOUZA. Greek Mythology. 3 vols. Petrópolis: Vozes, 2015.

PHILOSOPHY:

AQUINO, Tommaso d'. About education: the seven deadly sins. Translation: Luiz Jean Lauand. São Paulo: Martins Fontes, 2001.

BEAUVOIR, Simone. The Second Sex: facts and myths. 2 vols. Rio de Janeiro: Nova Fronteira, 1980.

PLATO. Phaedo. In: Great Thinkers. Translation: Jorge Paleikat and João Cruz Costa. São Paulo: Victor Civita, 1972.

PLATO. The Republic. Translation: Anna Lia A. A. Prado. São Paulo: Martins Fontes, 2006.

ARENDT, Hannah. What is Politics? Translation: Reinaldo Guarany. Rio de Janeiro: Bertrand Brasil, 1998.

ART:

QUILICI, Cassiano. Antonin Artaud: theater and ritual. São Paulo: Annablume/ Fapesp, 2004.

STANISLAVSKI, Constantin. Building a Character. Rio de Janeiro: Civilização Brasileira, 1986.

FILM:

Persona. Director: Ingmar Bergman. Sweden: 1966. B&W (85 min.).

ENEAGRAM:

@TheEnneagramInBusiness

Claudio Narajo and Ginger Lapid Bogda

#UNLEASHED

POST A PICTURE ON INSTAGRAM
HOLDING THE BOOK AND TAG

@institutodonadesi

@unleashedfoundation

@webook_publishing

www.institutodonadesi.com.br

www.webookpublishing.com

www.ingramcontent.com/pod-product-compliance
Lightning Source LLC
Chambersburg PA
CBHW072151200426
43209CB00052B/1112